AUTO-BIOGRAPH

This page enables you to compile a list of useful data on your car, so that whether you're ordering spares or just checking the tyre pressures, all the key information - the information that is 'personal' to your car - is easily within reach.

Registration number: ....

Model: ....

Body colour: ....

Paint code number: ....

Date of first registration: ....

Date of manufacture (if different): ....

VIN (or 'chassis') number: ....

Engine number: ....

Ignition key number: ....

Door lock key/s number/s: ....

Fuel locking cap key number (if fitted): ....

Alarm remote code (if fitted): ....

Alarm remote battery type: ....

Radio/cassette security code (if fitted): ....

Tyre size

Front: ....Rear: ....

Tyre pressure (normally laden)

Front: ....Rear: ....

Tyre pressure (fully laden)

Front: ....Rear: ....

Insurance

   Name and address of insurer:...

   ....

Policy number:

   ....

Modifications

   Information that might be useful when you need to purchase parts:..................................

   ....

   ....

Suppliers

   Address and telephone number of your garage and parts suppliers:..................................

   ....

First published in 1995 by Porter Publishing Ltd.

Porter Publishing Ltd.
The Storehouse
Little Hereford Street
Bromyard
Hereford HR7 4DE
England

British Library Cataloguing in Publication Data.

A catalogue record for this book is available from the British Library.

ISBN 1-899238-12-3

Series Editor: Lindsay Porter
Design: Martin Driscoll, Lindsay Porter and Lyndsay Berryman
Layout and Typesetting: Pineapple Publishing
Cover photograply: Jeremy Gale
Printed in England by The Trinity Press, Worcester.

Every care has been taken to ensure that the material contained in this Service Guide is correct. However, no liability can be accepted by the authors or publishers for damage, loss, accidents, or injury resulting from any omissions or errors in the information given.

Titles in this Series:

Absolute Beginners Service Guide
Caravan Owner's Manual & Service Guide
Classic 'Bike Service Guide
Diesel Car Engines Service Guide
Ford Escort & Orion Service Guide
Ford Fiesta Service Guide
Ford Sierra Service Guide
Land Rover Series I, II, III Service Guide

Land Rover Defender, 90 & 110 Service Guide
Mini (all models 1959-1994) Service Guide
MGB (including MGC, MGB GT V8 and MG RV8) Service Guide
Vauxhall Astra & Belmont Service Guide
Vauxhall Cavalier Service Guide
VW Beetle Service Guide

- With more titles in production -

Metro
Service Guide & Owner's Manual
by
Peter Wallage & Lindsay Porter

OIL AND WATER DON'T MIX

It is important to remember that even a small quantity of oil is harmful to water and wildlife. And tipping oil down the drain is as good as tipping it into a river. Many drains are connected directly to a river or stream and pollution will occur.

Each year the National Rivers Authority deals with over 6,000 oil related water pollution incidents. Many of these are caused by the careless disposal of used oil.

The used oil from the sump of just one car can cover an area of water the size of two football pitches, cutting off the oxygen supply and harming swans, ducks, fish and other river life.

Follow the Oil Care Code

◆ *When you drain your engine oil - don't oil the drain!* Pouring oil down the drain will cause pollution. It is also an offence.

◆ Don't mix used oil with other materials, such as paint or solvents, because this makes recycling very difficult.

◆ Take used oil to an oil recycling bank. Telephone FREE on 0800 663366 to find the location of your nearest oil bank, or contact your local authority recycling officer.

This book is produced in association with Castrol (U.K.) Ltd.

"Cars have become more and more sophistated. But changing the oil and brake fluid, and similar jobs are as simple as they ever were. Castrol are pleased to be associated with this book because it gives us the opportunity to make life simpler for those who wish to service their own cars. Castrol have succeeded in making oil friendlier and kinder to the environment by removing harmful chlorine from our range of engine lubricants which in turn prolong the life of the catalytic convertor (when fitted), by noticeably maintaining the engine at peak efficiency. In return, we ask you to be kinder to the environment too... by taking your used oil to your Local Authority Amenity Oil Bank. It can then be used as a heating fuel. Please do not poison it with thinners, paint, creosote or brake fluid because these render it useless and costly to dispose of."

Castrol (U.K.) Ltd

CONTENTS

Introduction

Over the years, I have run any number of cars, from superb classic cars and modern cars, to those with one foot in the breakers yard. And I know only too well that any car is only enjoyable to own if it's safe, reliable and basically sound - and the only way of ensuring that it stays that way is to service it regularly. That's why we have set about creating this book, which aims to show the owner interested in DIY car servicing that there's nothing to fear; you really can do it yourself!

Making It Easy! Porter Publishing Service Guides are the first books to give you all the service information you might need, with step-by-step instructions, along with a complete Service History section for you to complete and fill in as you carry out regular maintenance on your car over the months ahead. Using the information contained in this book, you will be able to:

◆ see for yourself how to carry out every Service Job, from weekly and monthly checks, right up to longer-term maintenance items.
◆ carry out regular body maintenance and rustproofing, saving a fortune in body repairs over the years to come.
◆ enhance the value of your car by completing a full Service History of every maintenance job you carry out on your car.

I hope you enjoy keeping your car in trim while saving lots of money by servicing your car yourself, with the help of this book. Happy motoring!

Lindsay Porter
Porter Publishing Ltd

Lindsay Porter

Peter Wallage

Acknowledgements

No book like this could possibly be a solo effort and my thanks are due to numerous people who have helped to make its final production possible. First to Lindsay Porter for the long hours he spent laying down the basic format for the series which arranges the jobs necessary in a logical, straight-forward sequence which makes it easy to follow even for the as-yet inexperienced enthusiast.

My thanks are due to David Ruston for lending me his car for the majority of photographs in this book and to Harry Lavender of Saracens Garage, Ashford, Kent, who provided a car for the rustproofing process together with the use of his hoist. The rustproofing was expertly carried out by Roger McNickle of Dinol (GB) Limited. More assistance came from Dunlop SP Tyres, from Sykes-Pickavant who kindly supplied almost all the high quality tools used here, and to David's Isopon who kindly supplied the expertise on body repair and finishing, and, of course, my thanks to Richard Price at Castrol whose advice and extensive knowledge of lubrication we value, and whose products we can unhesitatingly recommend.

Lastly my thanks to my wife Valerie for taking most of the photographs in this book and for the hours she spent at the computer putting coherence into my masses of notes and, of course, to anyone else who I might inadvertently have left out.

Peter Wallage

SPECIAL THANKS

The Publisher would like to thank: Rover Group Ltd for their advice and use of illustrative material - Gunsons for equipment, line drawings and advice - Nigel Newman Cars - Dinitrol for their kind assistance with Chapter 5 - and our good friends at Castrol for their continuing support, assistance and advice.

CHAPTER 1 - SAFETY FIRST!

You must always ensure that safety is the first consideration in any job you carry out. A slight lack of concentration, or a rush to finish the job quickly can easily result in an accident, as can failure to follow the precautions outlined in this Chapter. Whereas skilled motor mechanics are trained in safe working practices you, the home mechanic, must find them out for yourself and act upon them.

Remember, accidents don't just happen, they are caused, and some of those causes are contained in the following list. Above all, ensure that whenever you work on your car you adopt a safety-minded approach at all times, and remain aware of the dangers that might be encountered.

Be sure to consult the suppliers of any materials and equipment you may use, and to obtain and read carefully any operating and health and safety instructions that may be available on packaging or from manufacturers and suppliers.

PART I: IMPORTANT POINTS

Vehicle Off Ground

ALWAYS ensure that the vehicle is properly supported when raised off the ground. Don't work on, around, or underneath a raised vehicle unless axle stands are positioned under secure, load bearing underbody areas, or the vehicle is driven onto ramps, with the wheels remaining on the ground securely chocked to prevent movement.

ALWAYS ensure that the safe working load rating of any jacks, hoists or lifting gear used is sufficient for the job, and that lifting gear is used only as recommended by the manufacturer.

NEVER attempt to loosen or tighten nuts that require a lot of force to turn (e.g. a tight oil drain plug) with the vehicle raised, unless it is safely supported. Take care not to pull the vehicle off its supports when applying force to a spanner. Wherever possible, initially slacken tight fastenings before raising the car off the ground.

ALWAYS wear eye protection when working under the vehicle and when using power tools.

Working On The Vehicle

ALWAYS seek specialist advice unless you are justifiably confident about carrying out each job. The safety of your vehicle affects you, your passengers and other road users.

DON'T lean over, or work on, a running engine unless it is strictly necessary, and keep long hair and loose clothing well out of the way of moving mechanical parts. Note that it is theoretically possible for fluorescent striplighting to make an engine fan appear to be stationary - double check whether it is spinning or not! This is the sort of error that happens when you're really tired and not thinking straight. So...

...DON'T work on your car when you're over tired.

ALWAYS work in a well ventilated area and don't inhale dust - it may contain asbestos or other harmful substances.

REMOVE your wrist watch, rings and all other jewellery before doing any work on the vehicle - and especially when working on the electrical system.

DON'T remove the radiator or expansion tank filler cap when the cooling system is hot, or you may get scalded by escaping coolant or steam. Let the system cool down first and even then, if the engine is not completely cold, cover the cap with a cloth and gradually release the pressure.

NEVER drain oil, coolant or automatic transmission fluid when the engine is hot. Allow time for it to cool sufficiently to avoid scalding you.

ALWAYS keep antifreeze, brake and clutch fluid away from vehicle paintwork. Wash off any spills immediately.

TAKE CARE to avoid touching any engine or exhaust system component unless it is cool enough not to burn you.

Running The Vehicle

NEVER start the engine unless the gearbox is in neutral (or 'Park' in the case of automatic transmission) and the hand brake is fully applied.

NEVER run catalytic converter equipped vehicles without the exhaust system heat shields in place.

TAKE CARE when parking vehicles fitted with catalytic

converters. The 'cat' reaches extremely high temperatures and any combustible materials under the car, such as long dry grass, could be ignited.

Personal Safety

NEVER siphon fuel, antifreeze, brake fluid or other such toxic liquids by mouth, or allow contact with your skin. There is an increasing awareness that they can damage your health. Best of all, use a suitable hand pump and wear gloves.

BEFORE undertaking dirty jobs, use a barrier cream on your hands as a protection against infection. Preferably, wear thin gloves, available from DIY outlets.

WEAR GLOVES for sure when there is a risk of used engine oil coming into contact with your skin. It can cause cancer.

WIPE UP any spilt oil, grease or water off the floor immediately, before there is an accident.

MAKE SURE that spanners and all other tools are the right size for the job and are not likely to slip. Never try to 'double-up' spanners to gain more leverage.

SEEK HELP if you need to lift something heavy which may be beyond your capability. Don't forget that when lifting a heavy weight, you should keep your back straight and bend your knees to avoid injuring your back.

NEVER take risky short-cuts or rush to finish a job. Plan ahead and allow plenty of time.

BE METICULOUS and keep the work area tidy - you'll avoid frustration, work better and lose less.

KEEP children and animals right-away from the work area and from unattended vehicles.

ALWAYS tell someone what you're doing and have them regularly check that all is well, especially when working alone on, or under, the vehicle.

PART II: HAZARDS

Fire!

Petrol (gasoline) is a dangerous and highly flammable liquid requiring special precautions. When working on the fuel system, disconnect the vehicle battery earth (ground) terminal whenever possible and always work outside, or in a very well ventilated area. Any form of spark, such as that caused by an electrical fault, by two metal surfaces striking against each other, by a central heating boiler in the garage 'firing up', or even by static electricity built up in your clothing can, in a confined space, ignite petrol vapour causing an explosion. Take great care not to spill petrol on to the engine or exhaust system, never allow any naked flame anywhere near the work area and, above all, don't smoke.

Invest in a workshop-sized fire extinguisher. Choose the carbon dioxide type or preferably, dry powder but never a water type extinguisher for workshop use. Water conducts electricity and can make worse an oil or petrol-based fire, in certain circumstances.

DON'T disconnect any fuel pipes on a fuel injected engine while the ignition is switched on. The fuel in the line is under very high pressure - sufficient to cause serious injury. Remember that many injection systems have residual pressure in the pipes for days after switching off. Consult the workshop manual or seek specialist advice before carrying out any work.

Fumes

In addition to the fire dangers described previously, petrol (gasoline) vapour and the types of vapour given off by many solvents, thinners, and adhesives are highly toxic and under certain conditions can lead to unconsciousness or even death, if inhaled. The

risks are increased if such fluids are used in a confined space so always ensure adequate ventilation when handling materials of this nature. Treat all such substances with care, always read the instructions and follow them with care.

Always ensure that the car is out of doors and not in an enclosed space when the engine is running. Exhaust fumes contain poisonous carbon monoxide, even when the car is fitted with a catalytic converter, since 'cats' sometimes fail and don't function when the engine is cold.

Never drain petrol (gasoline) or use solvents, thinners adhesives or other toxic substances in an inspection pit as the extremely confined space allows the highly toxic fumes to concentrate. Running the engine with the vehicle over the pit can have the same results. It is also dangerous to park a vehicle for any length of time over an inspection pit. The fumes from even a slight fuel leak can cause an explosion when the engine is started. Petrol fumes are heavier than air and will accumulate in the pit.

Mains Electricity

Best of all, avoid the use of mains electricity when working on the vehicle, whenever possible. For instance, you could use rechargeable

tools and a DC inspection lamp, powered from a remote 12V battery - both are much safer. However, if you do use mains-powered equipment, ensure that the appliance is wired correctly to its plug, that where necessary it is properly earthed (grounded), and that the fuse is of the correct rating for the appliance is fitted. For instance, a 13 amp fuse in lead lamp's plug will not provide adequate protection. Do not use any mains powered equipment in damp conditions or in the vicinity of fuel, fuel vapour or the vehicle battery.

Also, before using any mains powered electrical equipment, take one more simple precaution - use an RCD (Residual Current Device) circuit breaker. Then, if there is a short, the RCD circuit breaker minimises the risk of electrocution by instantly cutting the power supply. Buy one from any electrical store or DIY centre. RCDs fit simply into your electrical socket before plugging in your electrical equipment.

The Ignition System

You should never work on the ignition system with the ignition switched on, or with the engine being turned over on the starter, or running.

Touching certain parts of the ignition system, such as the HT leads, distributor cap, ignition coil etc, can result in a severe electric shock. This is especially likely where the insulation on any of these components is weak, or if the components are dirty or damp. Note also that voltages produced by electronic ignition systems are much higher than those produced by conventional systems and could prove fatal, particularly to people with cardiac pacemaker implants. Consult your handbook or main dealer if in any doubt.

An additional risk of injury can arise while working on running engines, if the operator touches a high voltage lead and pulls his or her hand away on to a sharp, conductive or revolving part.

The Battery

Never cause a spark, smoke, or allow a naked light near the vehicle's battery, even in a well ventilated area. Highly explosive hydrogen gas will be given off as part of the charging process.

Battery terminals on the car should be shielded, since a battery contains energy and a spark can be caused by any metal object which touches the battery's terminals or connecting straps.

Before working on the fuel or electrical systems, always disconnect the battery earth (ground) terminal. (But before doing so, read the relevant **FACT FILE** in *Chapter 3* regarding saving computer and radio settings.)

When using a battery charger, care should be taken to avoid causing a spark by switching off the power supply before the battery charger leads are connected or disconnected. Before charging the battery from an external source, disconnect both battery leads before connecting the charger. If the battery is not of the 'sealed-for-life' type, loosen the filler plugs or remove the cover before charging. For best results the battery should be given a low rate trickle charge overnight. Do not charge at an excessive rate or the battery may burst.

Always wear gloves and goggles when carrying or when topping up the battery. Even in diluted form (as it is in the battery) the acid electrolyte is extremely corrosive and must not be allowed to contact the eyes, skin or clothes.

Brakes and Asbestos

Obviously, a car's brakes are among its most important safety related items. ONLY work on your vehicle's braking system if you are trained and competent to do so. If you have not been trained in this work, but wish to carry out the jobs described in this book, we strongly recommend that you have a garage or qualified mechanic check your work before using the car.

Whenever you work on the braking system's mechanical components, or remove front or rear brake pads or shoes: i) wear an efficient particle mask; ii) wipe off all brake dust from the brakes after spraying on a proprietary brand of brake cleaner (never blow dust off with compressed air); iii) dispose of brake dust and discarded shoes or pads in a sealed plastic bag; iv) wash your hands thoroughly after you have finished working on the brakes and certainly before you eat or smoke; v) replace shoes and pads only with asbestos-free shoes or pads. Note that asbestos brake dust can cause cancer if inhaled.

Brake Fluid

Brake fluid absorbs moisture rapidly from the air and can become dangerous resulting in brake failure. Castrol (U.K.) Ltd. recommend that you should have your brake fluid tested at least once a year by a properly equipped garage with test equipment and you should change the fluid in accordance with your vehicle manufacturer's recommendations or as advised in this book if we recommend a shorter interval than the manufacturer. You should buy no more brake fluid than you need, in smaller rather than larger containers. Never store an opened container of brake fluid. Dispose of the remainder at your Local Authority Waste Disposal Site, in the designated disposal unit, not with general waste or with waste oil.

Engine Oils

Take care to observe the following precautions when working with used engine oil. Apart from the obvious risk of scalding when draining the oil from a hot engine, there is the danger from contamination contained in all used oil.

Always wear disposable plastic or rubber gloves when draining the oil from your engine. i) Note that the drain plug and the oil are often hotter than you expect. Wear gloves if the plug is too hot to touch and keep your hand to one side so that you are not scalded by the spurt of oil as the plug comes away; ii) There are very real health hazards associated with used engine oil. In the words of one manufacturer's handbook "Prolonged and repeated contact may cause serious skin disorders, including dermatitis and cancer." Use a barrier cream on your hands and try not to get oil on them. Always wear gloves and wash your hands with hand cleaner soon after carrying out the work. Keep oil out of the reach of children; iii) NEVER, EVER dispose of old engine oil into the ground or down a drain. In the UK, and in most EC countries, every local authority must provide a safe means of oil disposal. In the UK, try your local Environmental Health Department for advice on waste disposal facilities.

Plastic Materials

Work with plastic materials brings additional hazards into workshops. Many of the materials used (polymers, resins, adhesives and materials acting as catalysts and accelerators) contain dangers in the form of poisonous fumes, skin irritants, and the risk of fire and explosions. Do not allow resin or 2-pack adhesive hardener, or that supplied with filler or 2-pack stopper, to come into contact with skin or eyes. Read carefully the safety notes supplied on the can, tube or packaging and always wear impervious gloves and goggles when working with them.

Jacks and Axle Stands

Throughout this book you will see many references to the correct use of jacks, axle stands and similar equipment - and we make no apologies for being repetitive. This is one area where safety cannot be overstressed - your life could be at stake!

Special care must be taken when any type of lifting equipment is used. Jacks are made for lifting the vehicle only, not for supporting it while it is being worked on. Never work under the car using only a jack to support the weight. Jacks must be supplemented by adequate additional means of support, positioned under secure load-bearing parts of the frame or underbody. Axle stands are available from most auto. parts stores. Drive-on ramps are limiting because of their design and size but they are simple to use, reliable and offer the most stable type of support. We strongly recommend their use.

Full details on jacking and supporting the vehicle will be found near the beginning of *Chapter 3.*

Fluoroelastomers

MOST IMPORTANT! PLEASE READ THIS SECTION!

If you service your car in the normal way, none of the following may be relevant to you. Unless, for example, you encounter a car which has been on fire (even in a localised area), subject to heat in, say, a crash-damage repairer's workshop or a vehicle breaker's yard, or if any second-hand parts have been heated in any way.

Many synthetic, rubber-like materials used in motor cars contain a substance called fluorine. These materials are known as fluoroelastomers and are commonly used for oil seals, wiring and cabling, bearing surfaces, gaskets, diaphragms, hoses and 'O' rings. If they are subjected to temperatures greater than 315 degrees C, they will decompose and can be potentially hazardous. Fluoroelastomer materials will show physical signs of

decomposition under such conditions in the form of charring of black sticky masses. Some decomposition may occur at temperatures above 200 degrees C, and it is obvious that when a car has been in a fire or has been dismantled with the assistance of a cutting torch or blow torch, the fluoroelastomers can decompose in the manner indicated above.

In the presence of any water or humidity, including atmospheric moisture, the by-products caused by the fluoroelastomers being heated can be extremely dangerous. According to the Health and Safety Executive, "Skin contact with this liquid or decomposition residues can cause painful and penetrating burns. Permanent irreversible skin and tissue damage can occur". Damage can also be caused to eyes or by the inhalation of fumes created as fluoroelastomers are burned or heated.

After a vehicle has been exposed to fire or high temperatures:

1. Do not touch blackened or charred seals or equipment.

2. Allow all burnt or decomposed fluoroelastomer materials to cool before inspection, investigations, tear-down or removal.

3. Preferably, don't handle parts containing decomposed fluoroelastomers, but if you must, wear goggles and PVC (polyvinyl chloride) or neoprene protective gloves whilst doing so. Never handle such parts unless they are completely cool.

4. Contaminated parts, residues, materials and clothing, including protective clothing and gloves, should be disposed of by an approved contractor to landfill or by incineration according to national or local regulations. Oil seals, gaskets and 'O' rings, along with contaminated material, must not be burned.

PART III: GENERAL WORKSHOP SAFETY

1. Always have a fire extinguisher of the correct type at arm's length when working on the fuel system.

If you do have a fire, DON'T PANIC. Use the extinguisher effectively by directing it at the base of the fire.

2. NEVER use a naked flame anywhere in the workplace.

3. KEEP your inspection lamp well away from any source of petrol (gasoline) such as when disconnecting a carburettor float bowl or fuel line.

4. NEVER use petrol (gasoline) to clean parts. Use paraffin (kerosene), white spirits, or a proprietary degreaser.

5. NO SMOKING. There's a risk of fire or of transferring dangerous substances to your mouth and, in any case, ash falling into mechanical components is to be avoided.

6. BE METHODICAL in everything you do, use common sense, and think of safety at all times.

CHAPTER 2 - BUYING GUIDE

In this Chapter, we show you how to go about buying a second hand car. We also look at which parts wear out, and we explain when they are likely to need replacement, so that whether you are giving your own car the once-over, or you're looking at a prospective purchase, you'll know what to expect; and we examine the best ways of buying parts for your pride and joy.

PART I: BUYING A SECOND-HAND CAR

In general, the safest - but also the most expensive - way of buying second hand is through a main dealer: NOT the same as a general second-hand dealer, whose standards are almost certain to be lower! We *strongly* recommend the use of HPI Autodata checks mentioned on page 110, because even main dealers can make 'mistakes', but once you've done that, and selected the main-dealer car you want, it's better to have an AA or RAC inspection carried out rather than carry out your own checks. But for many people, it's a question of saving money and buying privately, and that's what this Chapter is mainly about. But don't find yourself with the *worst* of both worlds...

Spot The Rogue Trader

One of the biggest dangers with buying privately is that you might encounter a real cheat: a trader masquerading as a private seller. Cars offered by such people are likely to be among the worst on offer, they may have had their mileometers tampered with and deep seated faults may have been cleverly concealed. Here's how to spot them:

• take note of the way traders often word their advertisements. Key phrases include: "a very clean car", "very straight", "a beautiful motorcar" and other glib phrases.

• when you telephone in response to an ad., *always* say, "I'm calling about the car..." If the person on the other end asks, "Which car?", put the 'phone down before the spiel starts.

• if you get past the telephone stage, take careful note of the attitude of the seller. Part-time, 'black economy' dealers often seem blase, even bored by the whole thing, and slicker than most private sellers.

• insist on looking at the Registration Document. If the seller isn't the registered keeper, why not?

How To Inspect A Used Vehicle

STAGE ONE: Even if you know very little about cars, you can root out the obvious no-hopers before arranging for a local main agent, AA or RAC inspection. The text in italics explains the problems.

• catch the light along all sides of the car. Can you see any ripples? Check for overspray inside wheel arches, inside engine bay and on tyres and trim. Does all the paint match? *All indicate poorly carried out crash repairs.*

• Look at the gaps between panels. Also, look very carefully inside the engine bay and inside the boot for evidence of rippling in the metal. Look low down, mainly in the vicinity of structural members. *Tell-tale signs of crash damage.*

STAGE TWO: If your car passes Stage One, look more closely at the bodywork - the most expensive part to repair.

• check the sills by lifting the carpets just inside the doors and also check the footwells, especially around the edges. *Rust!*

• look inside the engine bay especially at the tops of struts. *Check for corrosion.*

• check the bottoms of wings, the 'skirts' beneath front and rear bumpers and the tops of wing panels for corrosion. *Rust covered with filler will quickly burst through again.*

SPECIALIST SERVICE: It's hardly worth trying to check beneath a car without the use of a hoist. Leave it to the pro. inspection mentioned earlier, or see if you can persuade a local garage to lend or hire their hoist:

• check around spring mountings, the joints between floors and sills, all box-section 'chassis' members and anywhere that suspension components are fixed to the car's body structure.

• check all brake pipes and hoses. *Look for rubbing or corrosion.*

- look at the shock absorbers. *Fluid leakage means failure.*

- check the exhaust. *Look for rust, holes or patches.*

- examine each tyre carefully for bulges or splits. *Tyres worn more on one side than the other might mean that the car's tracking needs checking - easily adjustable - or it might indicate suspension damage, maybe from an accident.*

making it easy! If you are buying an older car which needs work doing to it, try making the owner an offer 'subject to MoT test'. Then, you can have the car tested as an inexpensive (though not necessarily complete) condition check.

Mechanical Components

- before starting up, remove the oil filler cap. *Grey sludge around the cap is a certain indicator that the engine is on its last legs.*

- pull out the dipstick. Is the oil level very low? Is the oil a dirty black and does it feel gritty between finger and thumb? *Not a well maintained car! Does it have droplets of water on it? Big problems! Probably a blown head gasket.*

- check inside the radiator cap (ONLY if the engine is cold!). Do you see anti-freeze colour? *Good!* Do you see rust? *Bad!* Do you see droplets of oil? *Disastrous! See previous paragraph.*

- start the car and note whether the starter motor sounds lively or whether it is struggling to keep up. *Could be duff battery; or tired starter motor.*

- undo and remove the oil filler cap again. (N.B. Most engines spray oil around in *copious* quantities. Ensure that you don't get covered!) *If oil mist chugs out, the engine bores are badly worn. Also...*

- ...look at the exhaust. Steam (especially in colder weather) and even water dripping out is no problem, although it should go away after the car has been driven. 'Rev' the engine, hard and several times. *If you see puffs or even clouds of black smoke (not grey steam), the engine is probably on the slippery slope.*

- does the oil pressure warning light flicker with engine cold? *Low oil pressure equals an engine rebuild?*

- bonnet open. Does the 'top' of the engine rattle on start up? *Mechanical tappets: adjustment needed.* If the rattle continues after 30 seconds, *the engine may need an expensive replacement camshaft. Hydraulic tappets: noise is always expensive!*

- rev the engine. Does it rattle in a deep, growly way, low down in the engine? *The big end and/or main bearings are gone - replacement engine time!*

Static Checks

- are the carpets wet? *water is leaking in. Windscreen seal leaks can often be cured easily. But if the car is old the screen surround may have corroded, requiring expensive welding. Alternatively, water coming in from beneath suggests that the car's lower structure has as much future as an old car park ticket. If water is leaking from the heater, remember that it can be expensive and tricky to replace.*

- seat rips can be a pain and devalue the car. *It can be difficult to find the right colour match on second hand seats.* Do your knees come up as your backside goes down. *The seat springing has gone.*

- can you live with headlining rips or severe discolouration? *It's difficult to clean easily and replacement is usually expensive.*

- take a *close* look at seat belts and mountings. *Life saver - and quite expensive to replace.*

- check that the heater works properly. *Or you'll end up hating the car!*

- take time to check every switch, accessory and electrical fitting on the car. *Replacements can be expensive.* Check that the stereo works - *and check that it's included with the car!*

- don't accept lame excuses when things don't work! *If things are so easy to fix, why haven't they been done already?*

- check the spare wheel and the condition (existence?) of the jack and toolkit. *More expense!*

- open and close windows and sunroof. *(Also look for stains around sunroof aperture - they can leak!)*

Finally, but perhaps most important of all, make sure that the person who is selling the car actually owns it!

- ask to see the Registration Document. *If it's not available it could be: the 'owner' has a) lost it; b) has it but it doesn't show the 'owner's' name because he is a trader; c) the car doesn't belong to the seller. If you can't see the Registration Document, walk away!*

- ask to see the owner's original purchase receipt and check that the car is owned by the 'owner' and is not subject to a finance agreement. See below. *IMPORTANT NOTE: You may be amazed to learn that, if you pay for a car that is subsequently found to belong to someone else, you will lose the car and the money!*

- check that the VIN (Vehicle Identification Number) shown on the Registration document is the same as those on the VIN plate riveted to the car. See "Fact File" later in this chapter for the precise location of these numbers. *If any of the numbers in these three locations are different, missing, or have obviously been tampered with, then under no circumstances consider buying the car unless the seller can provide an explanation, in writing, satisfactory to a third party, such as an AA or RAC inspector, or the Police!*

Spot The Rogue Car

Before buying *any* used car, check it out with HPI Autodata. (See Page 110.) A postal or telephone enquiry (cheques or credit card payments accepted) will (i) confirm that the vehicle details shown (make, model, colour, engine size, fuel type) are all correct, (ii) tell you if the vehicle is reported as stolen, or subject to an outstanding finance agreement, (iii) tell you if the vehicle has been logged as having a major insurance claim (not foolproof; many don't show up), (iv) identify vehicles which have had a registration plate change.

PART II: WHAT WEARS, AND WHEN

The following list provides a great way of checking what is *likely* to be worn on your Metro, and at what stage it is likely to need replacement - useful when checking your own car, or when buying another. Please bear in mind that the mileages shown are only intended as an approximation of the lifespan of each component. In real life, some will wear out faster and some slower, of course but the chart below provides a useful rough guide.

> **SAFETY FIRST!**
> *Read and take note of Chapter1, Safety First! and the Safety information in Chapter 3 before carrying out any of these checks.*

COMPONENT:	COULD NEED REPLACEMENT AT:	CHECKS OR SYMPTOMS:
Alternator	70,000 miles	Fails without warning
Battery	4 to 7 years (original); 1 to 4 (non-original)	Goes flat, even though disconnected
Brake Pads - Front	10 to 15,000 miles	See Job 43
Brake Shoes - Rear	35 to 40,000 miles	See Jobs 112 and 113
Clutch	Up to 75,000 normally	Check for slipping when pulling away, or hill climbing
Exhaust mountings	Rears go every year or two	Examine visually; twist manually
Exhaust pipe	(Rover parts) (non-original parts)	Up to 4 years 1 to 3 years Examine visually; listen for blowing
Shock absorbers (front) Shock absorbers (rear)	40,000 miles 40,000 miles	Clean off and look for oil leaks. Grasp and twist, looking for wear in bushes top and bottom.
Starter motor	100,000 miles	Turns engine slowly or fails to engage, *even though battery and connections in good condition*
Turbocharger (petrol)	100,000 miles	Prior warning symptoms: oil seal failure in turbo produces blue smoke from exhaust, once engine oil pressure rises.
Tyres (most models)	15 to 20,000 miles	Check visually, especially inside tyre walls and spare.

PART III - BUYING SPARES

One of the great advantages of DIY servicing is that you can choose which parts you buy, where you buy your parts, and how much you pay for them, whereas if the dealer services your car you buy their parts at their prices!

Of course, you must take care not to buy poor quality parts, but it's worth bearing in mind that many of the car makers' parts are the same as those available from 'independents'.

Buying The Right Parts

All manufacturers change the parts they use on the production line, often with startling frequency. The only way of ensuring that the parts you buy are the right ones for your car is to take your car's Vehicle Identification Number (VIN) and engine number with you when buying spares.

Main Dealers

Main dealers more than anyone else should be able to match your car's VIN number to the precise part you need, so have it to hand. This can also be the key to a more helpful approach by some Parts Department staff! Also, try to avoid calling on the parts department in the early mornings and other busy periods, and you may find that staff have more time to help you. Consumable items are almost certain to be too expensive from your main dealer. Try high street auto accessory stores or out-of-town Superstores for best prices.

Auto Accessory Stores

Local parts factors and big-name motor accessory shops can be extremely useful for obtaining servicing parts at short notice - many 'accessory' outlets open late in the evening, and on both days at weekends. You'll find that the high-street shops and Superstores will usually be open when you need them, their prices are usually the keenest of all, because they can buy-in in great quantities, and the quality of the parts is excellent from the best-known shops, since they use the same big-name manufacturers as many of the original car makers.

Buying Second-Hand

Purchasing any safety-related items second-hand - braking, steering or suspension parts - is something to avoid. That's not to decry buying second-hand altogether. Replacing a worn out distributor or carburettor, for instance, with a second-hand component that you know to be 'low mileage' can make a lot of sense. Equally, non-performance related items, such as wheel trims, interior trim and other interior parts can often be obtained at a fraction of the 'new' cost.

Reconditioned Parts

These are best obtained from reputable retail suppliers. When buying, always enquire about the terms of the guarantee. Don't buy if there isn't a good one! 'Exchange' alternators and starter motors are good value - but only buy from a reputable source.

Steering racks are invariably available as exchange items. Ensure that you rotate the operating shaft fully from lock to lock, feeling for any undue free play, roughness, stiffness, or 'notchiness' as you do so. Reject any units showing signs of any of these problems.

Tyres

We recommend buying only good quality radial ply tyres. Cheaper tyres rarely perform as well as top brands, even when they are the cheaper brand of a top manufacturer. Your car may steer more erratically, have less grip on cornering and braking and be noisier than if you pay the small extra amount required for top brand tyres - and they usually last longer, too. Remould tyres are available at lower initial cost, but life expectancy is not as long as with new tyres and we don't recommend them.

Shopping Around

If you want to buy good quality parts *and* save money, you must be prepared to shop around. Ring each of your chosen suppliers with a shopping list to hand, and your car's personal data, from the Auto-Biography at the front of this book, in front of you. Keep a written note of prices - including VAT, delivery etc - whether the parts are proper 'brand name' parts or not and - most importantly! - whether or not the parts you want are in stock. Parts expected 'soon' have been known never to materialise. A swivel pin in the hand is worth two in the bush. (Bad pun!)

FACT FILE: IDENTIFICATION NUMBERS

All manufacturers change the parts they use on the production line, often with startling frequency. The only way of ensuring that the parts you buy are the right ones for your car is to take your car's Vehicle Identification Number (VIN) and engine number with you when buying spares.

There are three main numbers you will need to know in order to buy parts and touch-up paint for your car. The VIN is your car's internationally unique number and tells your parts supplier *exactly* which model and year the car is. Quote the VIN whenever you buy spares for your car.

1. The Metro's VIN plate is positioned on the front or "slam"-panel of the engine and the number should be the same as that shown on your vehicle documents.

2. The engine number will be found on the engine block, adjacent to the alternator.

*INSIDE INFORMATION: If you need an exact paint colour match, you'll need the car's paint code number which should be **shown** on the VIN plate - although it's not there on every Metro! In these cases, take your car to your local paint factor and ask them to identify the colour. Most aerosol paints won't relate to this number, although at least one brand claims to be able to produce cans matched to your car's code colour, to special order. Alternatively, have your local paint factor mix a small quantity of matching paint for you.*

Please read the whole of the Introduction to this Chapter before carrying out any work on your car.

SERVICING YOUR CAR

CHAPTER 3 - SERVICING YOUR CAR

Everyone wants to own a car that starts first time, runs reliably and lasts longer than the average. And there's no magic about how to put your car into that category, it's all a question of thorough maintenance! If you follow the Service Jobs listed here or even if you have a garage or mechanic do it for you - you can almost *guarantee* that your car will still be going strong when others have fallen by the wayside... or the hard shoulder.

If you want your car to be as well looked after as possible, you'll follow the Jobs shown here, but if you don't want to go all the way, you can pick and choose from the most essential items in the list. But do bear in mind that the Jobs we recommend are there for some very good reasons:

◆ **body maintenance** is rarely included in most service schedules. We believe it to be essential.

◆ **preventative maintenance** figures very high on our list of priorities. And that's why so many of our service jobs have the word "Check..." near the start!

We think it's very important to keep things as straightforward as possible. And where you see this heading, you'll know there's an extra tip to help 'make it easy' for you!

The 'Catch-up' Service

When you first buy a used car, you never know for sure just how well it's been looked after. Even one with a full service history is unlikely to have been serviced as thoroughly as one with a Porter Manual Service History! So, if you want to catch-up on all the servicing that may have been neglected on your car, just work through the entire list of Service Jobs listed for the longest term servicing jobs listed in this Manual, and your car will be bang up to date and serviced as well as you could hope for. Do allow several days for all of this work, not least because it will almost certainly throw up a number of extra jobs - potential faults that have been lurking beneath the surface - all of which will need putting right before you can 'sign off' your car as being in tip-top condition.

The Service History

Those people fortunate enough to own a new car, or one that has been well maintained from new will have the opportunity to keep a 'Service History' of their car, usually filled in by a main dealer. Now you can keep your own complete record, using the tick list in the Appendix at the back of this book.

Your car's Service History will then be more complete and detailed than any manufacturer's service record, with the extra bonus that there is space for you to keep a record of all those extras: New tyres; replacement exhaust; extra accessories, so if your battery goes down only 11 months after buying it, you'll be able to look up where and when you bought it.

SAFETY FIRST!
SAFETY FIRST! information must always be read with care and always taken seriously. In addition, please read the whole of Chapter 1, Safety First! before carrying out any work on your car. There are many hazards associated with working on a car but all of them can be avoided by adhering strictly to the safety rules. Don't skimp on safety!

RAISING THE CAR

Raising The Car Before Working On It

Raising a Car - Safely!
You will often need to raise your car off the ground in order to carry out the Service Jobs shown here. To start off with, here's what you must never do - never work beneath a car held on a jack, not even a trolley jack. Quite a number of deaths have been caused by a car slipping off a jack while someone has been working beneath. On the other hand, the safest way is by raising a car on a proprietary brand of ramps. Sometimes, there is no alternative but to use axle stands. Please read all of the following information and act upon it!

When using car ramps:

(I) Make absolutely certain that the ramps are parallel to the wheels of the car and that the wheels are exactly central on each ramp.

Always have an assistant watch both sides of the car as you drive up. Drive up to the end 'stops' on the ramps but never over them!

Apply the hand brake firmly, put the car in first or reverse gear, or 'Park', in the case of an automatic.

I

(II) Chock both wheels remaining on the ground, both in front and behind so that the car can't move in either direction.

INSIDE INFORMATION: wrap a strip of carpet into a loop around the first 'rung' of the ramps and drive over the doubled-up piece of carpet on the approach to the ramps. This prevents the ramps from skidding away, as they are inclined to do, as the car is driven on to them.

On other occasions, you might need to work on the car while it is supported on an axle stand or a pair of axle stands. These are inherently less stable than ramps and so you must take much greater care when working beneath them. In particular:

II

Ensure that the axle stand is on flat, stable ground, never on a surface where one side can sink in to the ground.

Ensure that the car is on level ground and that the hand brake is off and the transmission in neutral.

(III) Raise the car with a trolley jack - invest in one if you don't already own one; the car's wheel changing jack is often too unstable. Place a piece of cloth over the head of the jack if your car is nicely finished on the underside. Ensure that the ground is sufficiently clear and smooth for the trolley jack wheels to roll as the car is raised and lowered, otherwise it could slip off the jack. (Illustration, courtesy Rover Group Ltd)

III. Jacking and supporting points

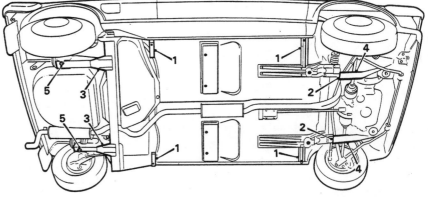

1. Wheelchange jack support bracket
2. Trolley jack lifting and support point (front)
3. Trolley jack lifting and support point (rear)
4. Jacking beam lifting point (front)
5. Jacking beam lifting point (rear)

(NB These last two are for professional workshop use only.)

III

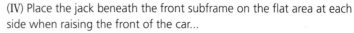

(IV) Place the jack beneath the front subframe on the flat area at each side when raising the front of the car...

(V) ...and place the axle stands beneath side outriggers as close to the chassis rail as you can get them, but NEVER under the engine or gearbox.

(VI) At the rear of the car, place the jack head, from the side, under the flat area just below the rear suspension arm. Place the axle stand under the rear outrigger close to the chassis rail.

(VII) Take care to locate the top of the axle stands only on a strong, stable part of the car's underside: you should never use a movable suspension part (because the part can move and allow the axle stand to slip) or the floor of the car (which is just too weak).

Just as when using ramps - only even more importantly! - apply the hand brake firmly once the car is supported on the axle stands, put the car in first or reverse gear (or 'Park', in the case of an automatic) and chock both wheels remaining on the ground, both in front and behind.

Be especially careful when applying force to a spanner or when pulling hard on anything, when the car is supported off the ground. It is all too easy to move the car so far that it topples off the axle stands. And remember that if a car falls on you, **YOU COULD BE KILLED!**

Whenever working beneath a car, have someone primed to keep an eye on you! If someone pops out to see how you are getting on every quarter of an hour or so, it could be enough to save your life!

Do remember that, in general, a car will be more stable when only one wheel is removed and one axle stand used than if two wheels are removed in conjunction with two axle stands. You are strongly advised never to work on the car with all four wheels off the ground, on four axle stands. The car would then be very unstable and dangerous to work beneath.

Before lowering the car to the ground, remember to remove the chocks, release the hand brake and place the transmission in neutral.

Raising The Car In An Emergency

SAFETY FIRST!
Wheel changing jacks can be dreadfully unstable! Take great care not to get any part of your body under the car when supported by one of these jacks.

It happens too often - a roadside puncture, probably in the dark, probably in the rain, the spare is flat, you don't know where the car jack is, or the wheelbrace, and even if you did you don't know where the jack should go, and the wheel nuts are far too tight to be shifted by that bit of bent rod they call a wheelbrace! If you've never done it before, changing a wheel is a daunting prospect, so practise the wheel-change routine at home, before the worst happens to you.

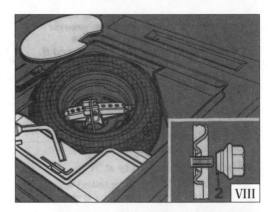

(VIII) START by finding where the jack and the wheelbrace are normally stowed. CHECK that the spare hasn't gone flat, because you check it every week, along with the other wheels/tyres. PREPARE by ensuring that in the boot and/or glovebox you have an old waterproof, something to kneel on, rag to clean your hands if necessary, but also protective gloves, and a torch. (Illustration, courtesy Rover Group Ltd.)

(IX) Wheel nuts should be done up to a specified degree of tightness, but all too often they're done up by a chap behaving like a gorilla with a toothache! Give yourself a better chance by buying one of these extendible wrenches, complete with the right-sized socket to fit your wheel nuts or bolts. Its superior strength and leverage will shift wheel nuts that the car-kit brace wouldn't even look at - it's an absolute 'must', not just for those who haven't got the strength of a raging gorilla but to replace that feeble wheel brace in the boot, for everyone!

In many instances, you will first have to lever off a wheeltrim - or plastic caps over the nuts that look like the real thing but are not! The car-kit wheelbrace might have a flattened end made for the job, otherwise find yourself perhaps a suitable screwdriver (keep it in the car) and lever carefully around the circumference of the trim: note where the tyre valve protrudes through, making a pencil mark if necessary. Once the wheeltrim is partly unclipped - it often needs vigorous levering, so watch that bodywork! - you may be better off doning your gloves and pulling.

(X) With the wheel still on the ground, loosen the wheel nuts. For your physical wellbeing you should always bear down on the wheelbrace, rather than pull it upwards - if you're stuck with that bent-rod car-kit brace, you'll probably need a length of pipe to slip over it to extend its leverage but it will probably be a struggle to keep it on the nut... If you try slackening the wheel nuts *after* you've raised the wheel, all you'll do it rotate the wheel, not the nut!

(XI) Make sure now that you know exactly where and how the car jack locates, and how it is operated: some might have a projection that plugs into a hole in the sill (you would first remove a rubber plug from the hole) others might straddle a particular stretch beneath the sill, some might lift both wheels clear of the ground from just one location, others might have a choice of two locations for front or rear wheel - if you are unsure, or if your handbook doesn't make it clear, seek the advice of your car dealer. Do it NOW, so that you'll know when you need it! (Illustration, courtesy Rover Group Ltd.)

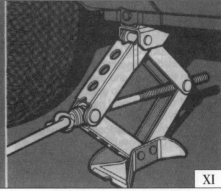

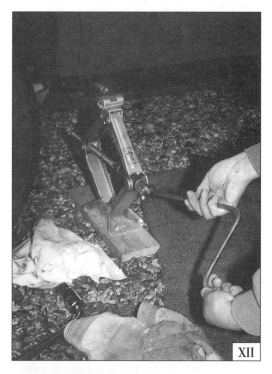

(XII) Also carry a piece of timber in the boot that can be placed beneath the jack to spread the load and prevent it from sinking into soft ground. Once the car is raised, have the handbrake on, and there are purpose-made chocks you can wedge each side of the wheel opposite to the one you are changing to guard against the car rolling. In an emergency, use any old pieces of wood or bricks that you can find. Wind the jack handle until the required wheel is clear of the ground, remembering that if the tyre is flat, you need enough clearance for a wheel with a fully pumped up tyre - do not put any part of your body beneath a car which is supported only on a jack.

(XIII) SAFETY FIRST! and INSIDE INFORMATION
Always place the spare wheel, or the wheel you've just removed, under the car: partly for safety to help guard against being crushed; partly so that if the car topples off the wheel-change jack (and they DO, especially on soft ground) you'll be able to reposition the jack and start again.

(XIV) Once the required wheel is clear of the ground, fully undo the nuts, leaving one 'at the top' until last so you can get your balance and a secure grip before lifting away the wheel. Fitting the replacement wheel is easier where studs and nuts are used, as on the Metro, because the studs give the wheel a positive location. Nip the nuts up finger-tight, then lower the wheel to the ground for final tightening, working diagonally, a little at a time, on each nut: do them up as tight as you can, using all your strength if it's the car-kit wheelbrace, slightly less than full strength if it's the extended wrench. (Note that the domed ends of the nuts fit against the wheel - see illustration VIII inset).

FACT FILE: ENGINE BAY LAYOUTS

Here is where you will find all the main servicing components in your Metro engine bay. Please note that the only major visual changes came at the end of 1984, when the clutch became cable operated (and so the hydraulic reservoir 'disappeared') and when, at the same time, the water radiator changed, so that the top hose became much larger and joined the radiator on the left instead of the right (when viewed from in front of the car).

I. ENGINE COMPARTMENT - manual gearbox

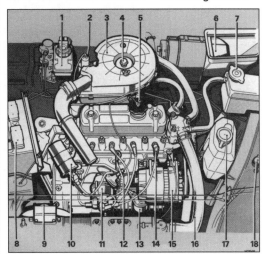

1. Brake fluid reservoir
2. PRE-1985 ONLY:
Clutch fluid reservoir
(not automatic)
3. Air cleaner
4. Carburettor piston damper
5. Engine oil filler cap
6. Heater air intake
7. Cooling system pressure relief cap and expansion tank
8. Battery
9. Fan motor
10. Coil
11. Distributor
12. Engine oil dipstick
13. Engine oil filter cartridge
14. Spark plug - No. 1 cylinder
15. Alternator
16. Top hose
17. Washer reservoir
18. Headlamp washer reservoir

II. ENGINE COMPARTMENT - automatic gearbox

1. Brake fluid reservoir
2. Air cleaner
3. Carburettor piston damper
4. Engine oil filler cap
5. Heater air intake
6. Cooling system pressure relief cap and expansion tank
7. Battery
8. Cooling fan motor
9. Engine oil dipstick
10. Coil
11. Distributor
12. Alternator
13. Spark plug - No. 1 cylinder
14. Engine oil filter
15. Top hose
16. Washer reservoir
17. Engine Number
NB See pre-1985 manual gearbox engine bay for location of clutch fluid reservoir on manual gearbox models before 1985.

III. ENGINE COMPARTMENT MG 1300, GTA and SPORT - manual gearbox

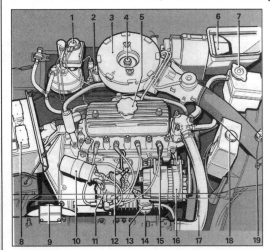

1. Brake fluid reservoir
2. Clutch fluid reservoir (PRE-'85)
3. Air cleaner
4. Carburettor piston damper
5. Engine oil filler cap
6. Heater air intake
7. Cooling system pressure relief cap and expansion tank
8. Battery
9. Fan motor
10. Coil
11. Distributor
12. Engine oil dipstick
13. Oil cooler (where fitted)
14. Engine oil filter cartridge
15. Spark plug - No. 1 cylinder
16. Alternator
17. Top hose (larger on later models)
18. Washer reservoir
19. Headlamp washer reservoir (early models only)

IV. ENGINE COMPARTMENT - MG TURBO

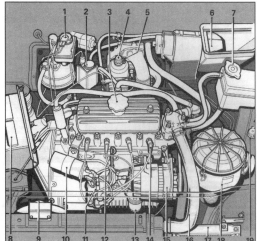

1. Brake fluid reservoir
2. Clutch fluid reservoir
3. Engine oil filler cap
4. Carburettor piston damper
5. Clamp
6. Heater air intake
7. Cooling system pressure relief cap and expansion tank
8. Battery
9. Fan motor
10. Coil
11. Distributor
12. Engine oil dipstick
13. Engine oil filter cartridge
14. Spark plug - No. 1 cylinder
15. Alternator
16. Top hose (larger on later models)
17. Oil cooler
18. Air cleaner
19. Headlamp washer reservoir (early models)

Every 500 miles, Weekly or Before Long Journeys, Whichever Comes First

These are the regular checks that you need to carry out to keep your car safe and reliable. They don't include the major Service Jobs but they should be carried out as part of every 'proper' service.

Every 500 miles - The Engine Bay

1A

1B

☐ **Job 1. Engine oil level.**

Check the engine's oil level with the car on level ground.

1A. On cars with manual transmission the dipstick is in front of the engine as you face the car. Lift out the dipstick, wipe it clean with a clean cloth, push it back in and lift it out again. Take a look at the level of the oil on the dipstick. You might have to do this three or four times before you can see a clear reading - the oil on the stick sometimes 'smears' as the stick is pulled out.

METROS WITH AUTOMATIC TRANSMISSION

On cars with automatic transmission the dipstick is behind the coil to the left of the engine as you face the car, beside the battery - see Fact File, above. Important Note! Accurate checking of the engine and automatic gearbox oil can be carried out *only* when the engine and gearbox are up to normal operating temperature. When the engine and gearbox are cold, use of the oil level dipstick should be confined to ensuring that the level is above the 'MIN' mark before running the engine and warming the engine and gearbox. Run the engine till it is up to normal operating temperature, then switch off the engine and allow it to stand for one minute. Withdraw the dipstick and wipe it clean with a clean cloth, push it back in and lift it out again. Take a look at the level of the oil on the dipstick. You might have to do this three or four times before you can see a clear reading - the oil on the stick sometimes 'smears' as the stick is pulled out.

1B. The oil level must be maintained above the 'MIN' mark on the dipstick. Approximately one pint, just over half a litre, will raise the level from the 'MIN' to the 'MAX' mark.

1C. On Austin models with a sheet metal rocker cover the oil filler cap is at the right hand end of the cover as you face the engine.

1D. On MG and Vanden Plas models with a cast aluminium rocker cover the oil filler cap is in the middle of the cover.

On all models, check the ground over which the car has been parked for evidence of oil or other fluid leaks. If any leaks are found, do not drive the car without first establishing where the leaks have come from - they could have come from a major failure in the braking system.

1C

1D

Our thanks are due to the Rover Group Limited for their kind permission to use a number of their line drawings. Copyright is retained by the company in question.

☐ Job 2. Clutch fluid level.

PRE-1985 METROS ONLY

2A. On most cars the clutch fluid reservoir is hidden beneath the air cleaner housing which has to be removed before the level can be checked and topped up. NOTE: In the case of Turbos, the clutch reservoir is not hidden by the air filter.

2B. With the air cleaner housing removed, wipe the top of the clutch reservoir clean, remove the cap and check the fluid level. If necessary, top up to the bottom of the filler neck. Make sure that the small vent hole in the cap is clear.

1985-ON METROS ONLY

From 1985-on, Metros were fitted with a cable-operated clutch. See Job 103 for lubrication details.

> **SAFETY FIRST!**
> *If clutch fluid should come into contact with the skin or eyes, rinse immediately with plenty of water.*

INSIDE INFORMATION: i) Check the ground on which the car has been parked, especially beneath the engine bay and each road wheel, for evidence of oil, clutch or brake fluid leaks. If any are found, investigate further before driving the car. ii) Clutch fluid will damage painted surfaces if allowed to come into contact. Take care not to spill any but, if there is an accident, refit the master cylinder reservoir cap and wash off any accidental spillage immediately with hot soapy water.

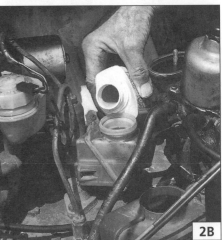

☐ Job 3. Brake fluid level.

> **SAFETY FIRST!**
> *i) If brake fluid should come into contact with the skin or eyes, rinse immediately with plenty of water. ii) It is acceptable for the brake fluid level to fall slightly during normal use, but if it falls significantly below the 'MIN' mark on the reservoir it indicates a leak or an internal seal failure. Stop using the car and seek **SPECIALIST SERVICE** immediately. iii) If you let dirt get into the hydraulic system it can cause brake failure. Wipe the filler cap clean before removing. iv) You should only ever use new brake fluid from an air-tight container. Old fluid absorbs moisture and this could cause the brakes to fail when carrying out an emergency stop or other heavy use of the brakes - just when you need them most and are least able to do anything about it, in fact.*

3A. The transparent brake fluid reservoir is on the left side of the bulkhead as you face the car. Wipe the top clean before removing the cap and be careful not to damage the wiring to the low-level warning switch. If necessary, top up the level to the 'MAX' mark on the side of the reservoir.

> *making it easy!* Should the push-on connectors become disturbed, don't worry because they can be replaced on either of the two terminals.

3B. Check the brake fluid level warning light. With the handbrake off - chock the wheels first - and the ignition switched on, depress the plastic plunger in the centre of the reservoir cap. The warning light on the dash should light up. If it does not, and the fluid level is satisfactory, stop using the car until you have had the circuit checked by a specialist.

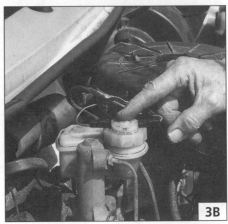

INSIDE INFORMATION: i) Check the ground on which the car has been parked, especially beneath the engine bay and each road wheel, for evidence of oil, clutch or brake fluid leaks. If any are found, investigate further before driving the car. ii) Brake fluid will damage painted surfaces if allowed to come into contact. Take care not to spill any but, if there is an accident, refit the master cylinder reservoir cap and wash off any accidental spillage immediately with hot soapy water.

FACT FILE: DISCONNECTING THE BATTERY

Many vehicles depend on a constant power supply from the battery and you can find yourself in all sorts of trouble if you simply disconnect the battery on those vehicles. You might find that the car alarm will go off, you could find that the engine management forgets all it has ever "learned" and the car will feel very strange to drive until it has re-programmed itself, and you could find that your radio refuses to operate again unless you key in the correct code. And if you've bought the car second-hand and don't know the code, you would have to send the set back to the manufacturer for re-programming. So, you must ensure that the vehicle has a constant power supply even though the battery is removed. To do so, you will need a

separate 12 volt battery supply. You *could* put a self tapping screw into the positive lead near the battery terminal before disconnecting it, and put a positive connection to your other battery via this screw. But you would have to be EXTREMELY CAREFUL to wrap insulation tape around the connection so that no short is caused. The negative terminal on the other battery would also have to be connected to the car's bodywork.

A better way is to use something like the Sykes-Pickavant Computer Saver shown here. Clip the cables to your spare battery and plug it into your cigarette lighter. (You may have to turn the ignition switch to the "Auxiliary" setting to allow the cigarette lighter to function.)

You have to hold in the red button on the Computer Saver while inserting it into the cigarette lighter, and if two green lights still

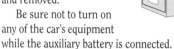

show after the button is released, you have a good connection and your battery can now be disconnected and removed.

Be sure not to turn on any of the car's equipment while the auxiliary battery is connected.

☐ **Job 4. Battery electrolyte**

SAFETY FIRST!

i) The gas given off by a battery is highly explosive. Never smoke, use a naked flame or allow a spark to occur in the battery compartment. Never disconnect the battery (it can cause sparking) with the battery caps removed. ii) Batteries contain sulphuric acid. If the acid comes into contact with the skin or eyes, wash immediately with copious amounts of cold water and seek medical advice. iii) Do not check the battery levels within half an hour of the battery being charged with a separate battery charger because the addition of fresh water could then cause the highly acid and corrosive electrolyte to flood out of the battery.

Many vehicles were fitted by the manufacturer with a 'sealed for life' battery, but it is possible that yours may have a 'normal' item, fitted by a subsequent owner. If yours is the former type, then no maintenance is required. This section relates to the common type of replacement battery.

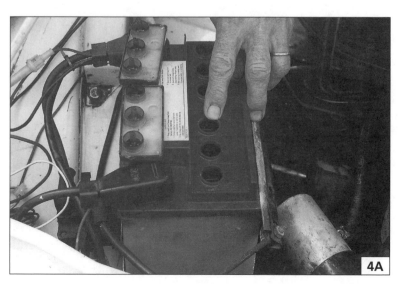

4A. The battery is mounted on a platform on the left hand side of the engine bay as you face the car. Remove the battery caps or covers and check the level of the electrolyte - the fluid inside each battery cell. The plates inside the battery should just be covered with electrolyte. If the level has fallen, top up with distilled water. NEVER use tap water, it can destroy your battery! After replacing the covers, dry off the top of the battery.

4B.INSIDE INFORMATION: i) Once water is mixed with acid inside the battery it won't freeze. So, in extremely cold weather, run the car (out of doors) so that you put a charge into the battery and this will mix the fresh water with the electrolyte, cutting out the risk of freezing and a cracked battery case. ii) Here's how to check the strength, or specific gravity, of the electrolyte. You place the end of a hydrometer into the battery electrolyte, squeeze and release the rubber bulb so that a little of the acid is drawn up into the transparent tube. The float, or floats, inside the tube (small coloured beads are sometimes used) give the specific gravity. If a battery goes flat because the car has been left standing for too long, use a small battery charger to re-charge the battery, following the maker's instructions and disconnecting the battery on the car first. A battery that goes flat too rapidly can be checked by a garage - they may well check the specific gravity of the electrolyte in each cell in order to establish whether one or more has failed but, since garages often tell you that you need a new battery anyway, it might be worth investing in a hydrometer and testing the cells yourself. Otherwise, you could try disconnecting the battery and seeing if it still goes flat. If not, suspect a wiring fault allowing the current to drain away but do be aware that some car alarms will drain a battery in around a week. They are designed primarily for cars that are used almost every day, rather than those that may not be used so often.

4B

making it easy! 4C. If the terminals are furry with crystals or corroded, don't spend hours sanding them: clean them by pouring a kettle of hot water over them. Dry the battery top and coat the terminals with Vaseline (petroleum jelly). Keep the water out of the battery cells, away from other components and wash any dislodged 'furr' away from the car's bodywork.

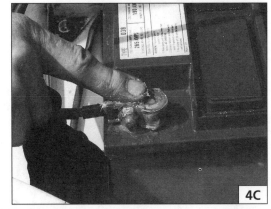

4C

4D. Check security of the battery clamp. Check inside the clamps, too, especially if the outsides show signs of corrosion. After washing off, scrape back to shiny metal.

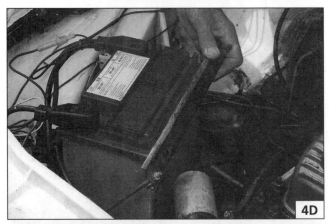

4D

 **Job 5. Washer reservoir.**

5. On non-turbocharged cars, the reservoir for the windscreen washers is situated on the inner wing on the right hand side as you face the car. On turbo models the reservoir for the combined windscreen and rear window washer is situated in the luggage compartment. Check the level and top up if necessary. See Job 9 for details of locations.

Remember that in cold weather a stronger concentration of washer fluid will help to prevent the washer system from freezing up. Check the recommended dilution on the package.

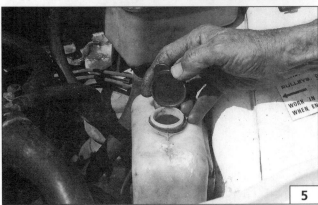

5

☐ Job 6. Cooling system level.

SAFETY FIRST!
i) The coolant level should only be checked WHEN THE SYSTEM IS COLD . If you remove the pressure cap when the engine is hot, the release of pressure can cause the water in the system to boil and spurt several feet into the air with the risk of severe scalding. ii) Take precautions to prevent ant-freeze coming into contact with the skin or eyes. If this should happen, rinse immediately with plenty of water and, if necessary, seek immediate medical assistance.

6A. Carry out a visual check on all cooling system and other hoses in and around the engine bay for leaks.

6B. The cooling system expansion bottle is on the inner wing on the right as you stand in front of the car. If necessary, top up the system with a mixture of 50% anti-freeze and water to the level mark on the expansion bottle.

☐ Job 7. Heater intake box.

7A. The heater air intake box is on the bulkhead behind the coolant expansion tank. Check inside that it is free from leaves or other debris that could block the air flow.

7B. INSIDE INFORMATION: Underneath the heater intake box is a water drain flap valve. Make sure it is not seized and that the rubber has not gone hard. If water gathers in the box because this flap has filled with debris, corrosion will set in.

☐ Job 8. Check horn.

8. Try the horn button. If the horn fails to sound, check the electrical connections to the horn itself. The horn is mounted on the inner wing in front of where the washer reservoir bottle is situated on most cars.

SPECIALIST SERVICE: Horn wiring and connections can be more complex than they appear at first. For instance, on some models, both terminals at the horn should be 'live'! If there is no obvious problem with the wiring connections, have the horn, the circuitry and the switch checked over by a specialist.

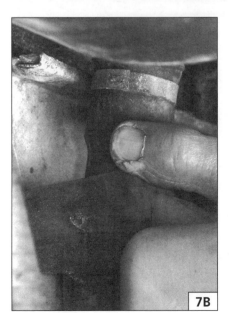

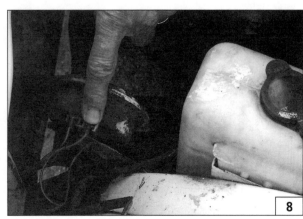

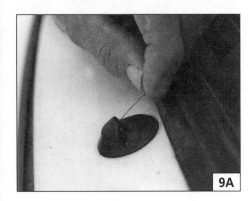

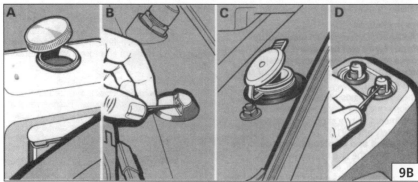

Every 500 miles - Around the Car

☐ **Job 9. Windscreen washers.**

9A. Check the operation of the windscreen washers and, on some models, the rear screen washer. If one of the jets fails to work, check that the pipe has not come adrift and then check with a pin that the jet is clear. The angle of the jet can be adjusted with a pin. It should hit the screen just over halfway up.

9B. Most Metros have their reservoir in the engine bay (A) but the Turbos have theirs in the rear luggage compartment. Rear washer jets are adjusted as for fronts (B). Where headlamp washers are fitted, there is a separate reservoir in the engine bay (C) and the jets (D) are adjusted in a similar way.

☐ **Job 10. Windscreen wipers.**

10A. Lift the wiper blade away from the screen and examine the edge for damage or waviness which indicates that it is worn out. Give each blade a wipe with clean methylated spirit (industrial alcohol).

10B. If the blade needs renewing it lifts off the wiper arm when you depress a small catch at the end of the arm, on earlier models.

10C. On later models, you press the retaining lever on the wiper blade (unit) and slide the blade along the arm in the direction arrowed.

☐ **Job 11. Tyre pressures.**

11. Use a reliable pressure gauge to check the pressure in each tyre, including the spare. Always check pressures with the tyres cold, never just after using the car which warms up the tyres and increases their pressure.

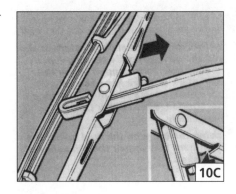

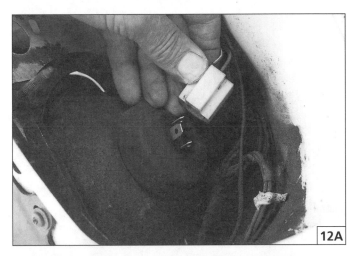

12A

☐ Job 12. Check headlights.

Check the operation of the headlights on both full and dipped beam. If one beam fails to work on either side the bulb has probably failed. IMPORTANT NOTE: On some models, the sidelights are fitted to the headlight bowl. For the separate-type, see Job 13.

12A. To gain access to the headlight bulb, first remove the terminal connector. This is a three-prong terminal and the connector cannot be replaced the wrong way round.

12B. After removing the rubber cover, turn and remove the spring clip which holds the bulb in position. Note, if the bulb feels loose, gently bend the clip slightly before replacing it, to give it more grip.

12C. Lift out the bulb to examine the filaments. Hold the bulb only by the metal part. Particularly on quartz-halogen bulbs, finger marks on the glass envelope will severely detract from the light output and could cause the bulb to blow.

INSIDE INFORMATION: If you do accidentally get 'finger-prints' on the bulb, wipe it clean with methylated spirits on a clean cloth or paper tissue.

12B

12D. To gain access to the headlight aim adjustment, undo the screws and remove the headlight surround from the front of the car.

12E. Adjust the headlight aim by two screws at the top of the light unit. **SPECIALIST SERVICE:** It is not possible to set the aim of the headlights accurately at home. In *Chapter 7, Getting Though the MoT,* we show how to trial-set your headlights before going to the MoT Testing Station (in the UK). This method is only suitable if you are going to have the settings re-checked by a garage with proper beam checking equipment.

12C

12D

12E

500 MILE/WEEKLY SERVICE

☐ Job 13. Check front sidelights and direction indicators.

IMPORTANT NOTE: On some cars, the front sidelights and indicator lights are integral with the headlight surround and are checked at the same time as carrying out Job 12 after removing the headlight cover.

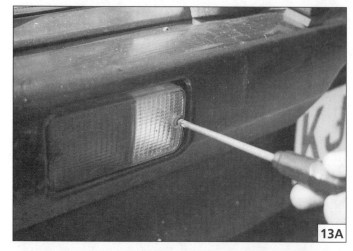

13A. On cars with separate front sidelights and indicators, to gain access to the bulbs, undo the two screws holding the lens in position on the front bumper.

13B. Ease the lens gently out of position. If it sticks because of road dirt, clean round it gently.

INSIDE INFORMATION: Do not lever it out with a screwdriver as this is likely to break it.

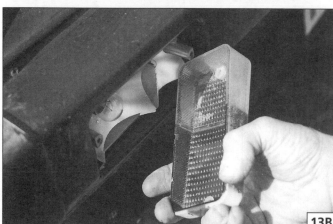

13C. Bulbs are removed by pushing them in, twisting anti-clockwise and pulling out, but watch your fingers - there is often very little to grip. If the reflector and lens are dirty, wash them in warm soapy water and dry. Clean reflectors and lenses make a big difference to the light output!

INSIDE INFORMATION: If the bulb won't budge, try wrapping a piece of masking tape around the bulb to provide extra grip.

☐ Job 14. Check side marker indicators.

14A. To gain access to a side indicator bulb, first disconnect the two electrical connections under the bonnet just inside the inner wing.

14B. Then ease the bulb holder from behind the side indicator light and pull the wire down far enough to be able to get at the bulb.

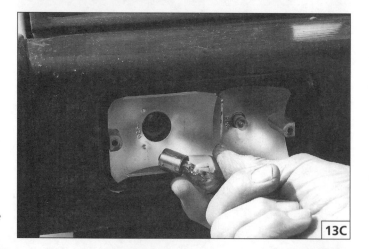

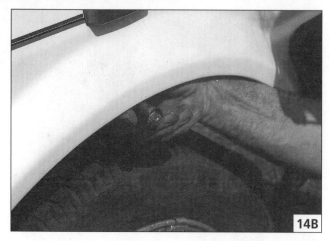

□ **Job 15. Check rear sidelights, indicators and reverse light.**

15A. To gain access to the rear light cluster, first remove the trim panel from above the combined lens.

15B. After taking off the top trim panel, remove the four screws that hold the rear light cluster lens.

15C. On the combined stop and rear light, note that the bulb has offset pins so that it cannot be replaced the wrong way round. If the reflectors and lens are dirty, wash them in clean soapy water and dry.

□ **Job 16. Check rear fog lights.**

16A. Remove the lens from the rear fog lights by undoing the two screws holding it in the rear bumper.

16B. If the lens does not lift out easily, clean round it. Do not lever it with a screwdriver as this is likely to break it.

INSIDE INFORMATION: When you lift the lens out, be careful because the same screws retain the reflector. If the reflector and lens are dirty, wash them in warm soapy water and dry.

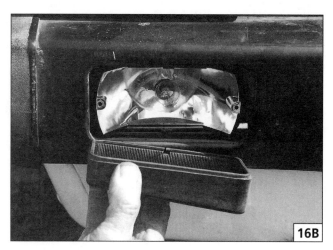

500 MILEWEEKLY SERVICE

☐ Job 17. Check rear number plate light.

The rear number plate light is tucked up under the rear bumper.

17A. To gain access on some models, squeeze the grips and ease the light downwards. Turn the bulb holder anti-clockwise to release it from the light. (Illustration, courtesy Rover Group Ltd.)

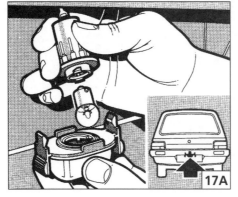

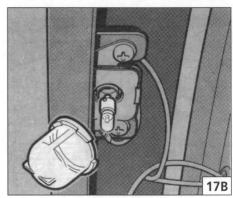

17B. On other models, to gain access to the bulb, press the lens and turn it anti-clockwise. (Illustration, courtesy Rover Group Ltd.)

☐ Job 18. Check luggage compartment light (where fitted).

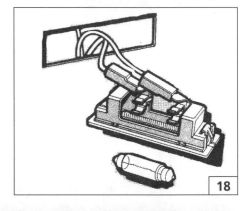

18. To gain access to the bulb, gently ease the light from its location with a screwdriver. The bulb may be a normal type, or a tubular festoon type which just clips into position. If the bulb appears to be sound, and the fuse has not blown, and if the light refuses to light, suspect a sticking pin switch located on the rim of the luggage compartment. If this appears to be free, and the light still does not light, the switch should be checked (see 19B). Otherwise seek the advice of an auto electrician. (Illustration, courtesy Rover Group Ltd.)

☐ Job 19. Check interior light.

19A. To gain access to the bulb, ease the light gently from its location with a screwdriver. The bulb may be a normal type, or a tubular festoon type which just clips into position.

19B. If the bulb appears to be sound, and the fuse has not blown, then if the light refuses to light suspect a sticking courtesy switch in the door post. If this appears to be free, (i.e. can be pushed in and out) unscrew it and replace it with a new one, from your Rover dealer. If the light still does not light, seek the advice of an auto electrician.

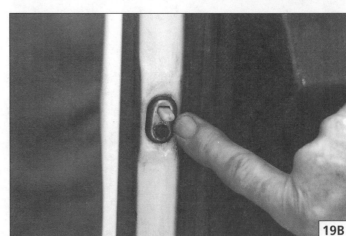

INSIDE INFORMATION: If a complete 'set' of bulbs fails to operate (and especially if other electrical components fail at the same time) check the fuses before suspecting any other fault. If a replacement fuse blows, you probably have a circuit fault. Seek SPECIALIST SERVICE immediately. If, on later model cars, the headlight dipped beam still fails to work after the bulb and fuse have been checked, the 'dim-dip' resistor may have failed. Seek SPECIALIST SERVICE.

FACT FILE: FUSES

I. The main fuses are situated beneath the switch panel under the fascia by the side of the steering wheel. On older models, you undo two screws (one arrowed; the other at the other end of the panel) and pivot the panel down. On later models, the fuses are in the same position but have a cover over them which is released by using a coin in two turnbuckles. Some models also have line fuses in the wiring.

II. On earlier models, the fuses are on the inside of the switch panel together with the flasher units for the direction indicators and hazard warning indicators. Important Note: To avoid overloading the electrical circuits and the subsequent possibility of fire, never fit a fuse that exceeds the recommended amperage for each location listed.

III. The position of the fuses on earlier models. (Illustration, courtesy Rover Group Ltd.)

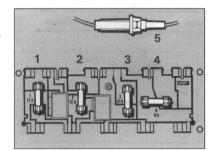

IV. The position of the fuses under the fascia on later models. Note: Spare fuses are located in the top row, above the numbered rows. Ensure that a spare fuse of each rating is carried. Some fuses are colour coded as follows: Violet, 3 amp; Tan, 5 amp; Red, 10 amp; Blue, 15 amp; Green, 30 amp. (Line drawing courtesy Rover Group)

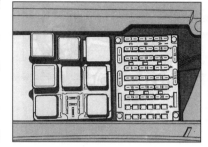

These units not operating:	With ignition switch in postion:	Indicates a blown fuse number:
Direction indicators, stop and reverse lights, heated rear window and warning light.	'I'	1 (17 amp)
Interior light, hazard warning lights, and cigar lighter.	ANY	2 (12 amp)
Sidelights, rear and number plate lights, panel lights, switch illumination lights.	ANY	3 (8 amp)
Heater control, wiper motor, tailgate washer motor.	'I' or 'II'	4 (8 amp)
Rear fog light.	'I' or 'II'	5 (line fuse, 15 amp)
Wiper motor, washer motor, heater motor.*	'I' or 'II	5 (line fuse, 35 amp)
Fuel pump. (MG Turbo only)	'II'	5 (line fuse, 35 amp)

* Note: The wiper motor, washer motor and heater motors are protected by two fuses. If these units are still inoperative after renewing the line fuse, check fuse number 4 on the main panel. Line fuses (5) are located as follows: For the rear fog lights, it is behind the switch panel; the common fuse for the wiper motor, washer motor and heater motor is in the engine compartment on the right-hand wing valance; for the fuel pump on the MG Turbo, it is in the engine compartment on the left-hand wing valance.

These units not operating:	Check fuse No:	Fuse rating:
Heated rear screen.	A1	15 amp
Front window motors, if fitted.	A2	30 amp
Interior lights and central door locking.	A3	15 amp
Instruments, turbo units.	A4	5 amp
Indicators and hazards	A5	10 amp
Cigar lighter	A5	10 amp
Left-hand side and rear lights	B1	5 amp
Right-hand side and rear lights number plate lights and switch illumination.	B2	5 amp
Left-hand headlight dipped beam.	B3	10 amp
Right-hand headlight dipped beam.	B4	10 amp
Left hand headlight main beam.	B5	10 amp
Right-hand headlight main beam.	B6	10 amp
Radio.	C1	3 amp
Heater blower motor.	C2	15 amp
Windscreen wiper and washers.	C3	15 amp
Rear fog lights.	C4	5 amp
Stop and reverse lights and indicators.	C5	10 amp
Rear screen wiper and washer	C6	15 amp
Cooling fan, non-turbo cars.	C7	15 amp
Cooling fan MG Turbo.	C7	25 amp

☐ **Job 20. Valet bodywork.**

Wash the paintwork and glass with water and a suitable car detergent taking care not to get 'wax-wash' on the glass. Finish by washing the wheels and tyre walls. Leather the paintwork dry and then polish. Use a separate leather on the glass to avoid transferring polish from the paintwork. Use a proprietary glass cleaner and a soft cloth to get the windows sparkling clean.

☐ **Job 21. Vacuum interior.**

Use a vacuum cleaner with a flexible hose to clean the upholstery and carpets. If you haven't got a suitable vacuum cleaner, use one at a garage valeting station. Mains-models are much more powerful than the small type which plug into the car's cigar lighter socket, which are fairly useless!

Every 1,500 miles - or Every Month, Whichever Comes First

Every 1,500 miles - Around the Car

☐ **Job 22. Check tyre treads.**

22. Check the tyres (including the spare) for tread depth, using a depth gauge and note that, in the UK, the minimum legal tread depth is 1.6 mm. Tyres are not at their safest at that level and you may want to replace them earlier. Also check both sides of each tyre for uneven wear, bulges or other damage to the side walls. Raise each wheel of the ground, using an axle stand, otherwise you won't be able to see the inside of each tyre properly, nor will you be able to check that part of the tyre which is in contact with the ground.

SAFETY FIRST!
Tyres which show uneven wear tell their own story, if only you know how to speak the language! If any tyre is worn more on one side than another, consult your main dealer or a tyre specialist. It probably means that your suspension or steering is out of adjustment - probably a simple tracking job but conceivably symptomatic of suspension damage, so have it checked. If a tyre is worn more in the centre or on the edges, it could mean that your tyre pressures are wrong but, once again, have the car checked. Incorrectly inflated tyres wear rapidly, can cause the car's handling to become dangerous and can even cause the car to consume noticeably more fuel. When checking your tyres, don't forget to include the spare.

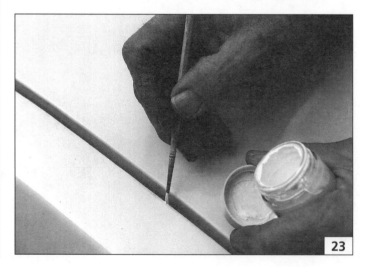

☐ **Job 23. Touch-up paintwork.**

23. Touch-up stone chips with a small brush to prevent rust. If rust is already showing, treat first with a proprietary rust killer, following the instructions on the package. Allow new paint to harden before polishing.

Every 1,500 miles - Under the Car

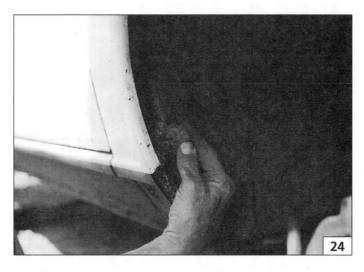

24

☐ **Job 24. Clean mud traps.**

24. If the car is particularly muddy underneath, hose it off, preferably with a power jet hose at a garage or, if only lightly muddy, scrape and brush off the dry mud. Pay particular attention to the areas under the wheel arches. You may find it easier to remove the wheels to carry out this job.

Every 3,000 miles - or Every Three Months, Whichever Comes First

Every 3,000 miles - The Engine Bay

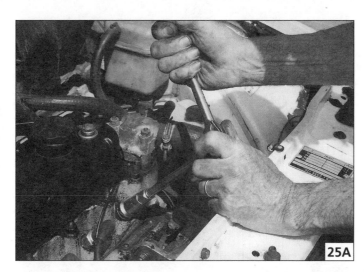

25A

☐ **Job 25. Adjust spark plugs.**

25A. Remove the high tension leads from the plugs after numbering them to make sure you get them back in the right firing order.

making it easy! Use a socket set with a proper plug spanner which has a rubber insert to avoid damage to the plug insulators. Some special plug sockets also have an internal circlip to hold the plug when you lift the socket away. You can also get special 'wobble' extensions for your socket set which have a curve on the squared end so that the extension can rock slightly in the socket to avoid putting side pressure on the plug if you don't hold the extension quite straight.

25B. Check the sparking plugs to make sure they are in acceptable condition (see the colour illustrations on page 65). Also check that the end nut (arrowed) to which the plug cap clips, is tight - use pliers.

25B

25C. Clean the plug electrodes with a brass brush - not a steel one - applied vigorously. After cleaning, check that i) the round screw-on terminal for the HT leads is tight - check it with a pair of pliers - and ii) that the gap is correct. - see *Chapter 8, Facts and Figures.* In most cases, the gap will need closing and the best way to do this is to tap the earth electrode lightly with a pair of pliers or similar tool, checking the gap after each tap. If the gap is too small, open it by levering the earth electrode away from the centre electrode taking great care not to damage the centre electrode nor its insulation. When the gap is correct, the appropriate feeler gauge should slide in easily without being loose. If in doubt, renew the plugs. Running with old worn plugs is false economy but, having said that, don't change them just for the sake of it. Look for evidence of burning, bad staining or the earth electrode wearing so thin that it is in danger of

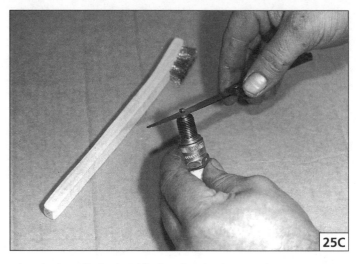

breaking off. Finally, make sure the threads are clean, screw the plugs in the cylinder head by hand and tighten to the recommended torque See *Chapter 8, Facts and Figures.* Carry out the next job before replacing the HT leads.

making it easy! An easy way of numbering the HT leads is to use dabs of typewriter correction fluid, marking the leads with one dab, two dabs and so on, with number one at the front. You need only mark the leads 1 to 3, the unmarked one must be 4. Alternatively, number them with strips of masking tape with the figures written on, or you can buy clip-on numbers. Never assume that the gap on new plugs is correct. They are set to an average gap at the factory, but that may or may not be the right one for your engine.

☐ **Job 26. Check HT circuit.**

26A. Clean the HT leads and check for signs of surface cracking, and loose connection where the lead fits on to the plug connector and into the distributor cap.

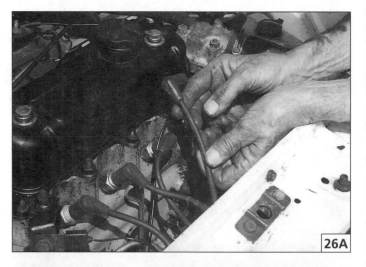

26B. Clean the distributor cap inside and out and check for any signs of 'tracking', burnt lines where carbon has lodged in a faint crack to provide a short circuit for the HT current. Any signs of tracking means that the cap could let you down with poor starting and bad running at any time as well as increasing your fuel consumption. Check also that the centre carbon brush still has plenty of length and that it is springy enough to bear on the centre of the rotor arm. Check the studs in the distributor cap for burning. Light burning can be cleaned up with fine glasspaper (better than emery paper because it does not leave any conducting dust behind). Check that the rotor arm fits firmly and not loosely on the centre cam of the distributor and check the end of it for burning. Again, light burning can be cleaned up but severe burning of either the cap studs or the rotor arm means renewal. Clean and check the insulated top of the coil. Again, tracking here can cause poor starting and misfiring.

INSIDE INFORMATION: If you have to renew either the HT leads or the distributor cap, renew the leads one at a time so you don't get them out of order. With a new cap, compare the position of the connection for number 1 cylinder with the old cap, using the depression where it locates on the body of the distributor as a reference point.

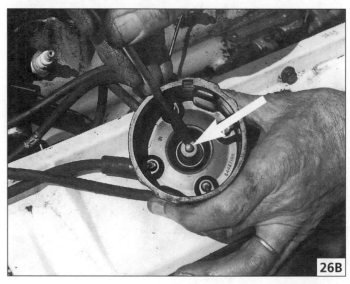

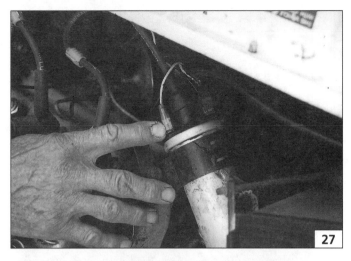

☐ Job 27. Check ignition LT circuit.

27. Check that the connections of the low-tension circuit at the coil and the distributor are firm.

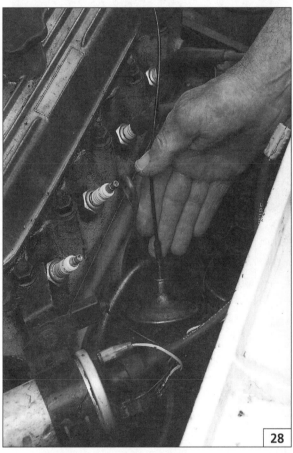

☐ Job 28. Distributor vacuum advance/retard pipe.

28. Check that the vacuum advance and retard pipe from the distributor to the carburettors is in good condition and fits tightly to its connectors.

☐ Job 29. Check cb points.

CONTACT BREAKER IGNITION ONLY

making it easy! Many mechanics swear that the only way to check or change a Metro's points is by taking off the distributor. Undo the TWO bolts, holding the clamp plate to the block. DON'T disturb the pinchbolt illustrated in 30A.

29A. The distributor on a Metro engine is tucked away down the front of the engine behind the radiator where it is difficult to get at for anything other than checking the points gap and the points condition. You are not changing the points at this stage, that comes in a later service schedule. For now, unless they are burnt, you will just be examining them and setting the gap.

29B. With the ignition turned off, open the points with a small screwdriver (29B.2). If they look burnt, it is a sign that they need renewing. You will probably need a new capacitor as well, as burnt points can be a sign of a faulty capacitor. We show you how to fit these in Job 71.

NOTE: On cars fitted with electronic ignition there are no points inside the distributor and no adjustment or maintenance is necessary other than checking the timing if the distributor has been moved. (Illustration, courtesy Rover Group Ltd.)

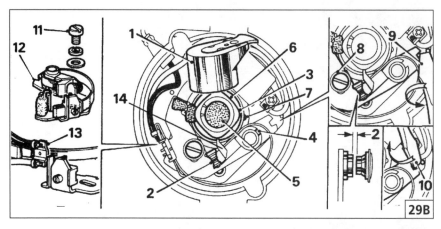

ELECTRONIC IGNITION ONLY

29C. You should also take this opportunity to lubricate the distributor. This is the electronic ignition distributor. After removing the distributor cap, you pull the rotor arm (1) and the dust shield (2) together. Add *a few drops* of light oil to the top of the rotor shaft (3) and a *few* more drops through the base plate (4) to lubricate the mechanical advance mechanism beneath. (Illustration, courtesy Rover Group Ltd.)

OLDER METROS AND 1.0 LITRE ENGINES AND VANS FROM 1985-ON

LUCAS DISTRIBUTORS: In the case of distributors that are fitted with points, you must take great care not to get grease or oil on the faces of the points. Smear just a trace of high melting point grease on the faces of the centre cam (29B.6) and allow a few drops of general lubricating oil to run down inside the points base plate (29B.7) to lubricate the mechanical advance and retard mechanism. If the car has been badly neglected from a service point of view, it does no harm to squirt a small amount of releasing fluid down under the baseplate before oiling to free the advance and retard mechanism should it have been sticking. An advance and retard mechanism which sticks or is jerky in operation can cause your engine to lose power. Should you get any oil or grease on the faces of the points, clean it off with methylated spirit (industrial alcohol).

> **SAFETY FIRST!**
> *But make sure all the methylated spirit has completely evaporated away before attempting to start the engine. All contact breaker distributors spark slightly at the points and, should this happen with methylated spirit vapour trapped inside, it could explode like a small bomb!*

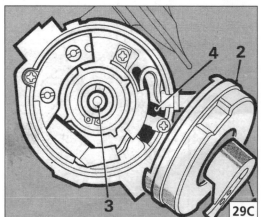

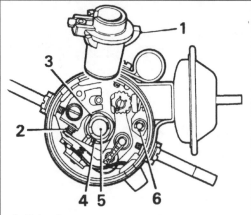

1. Rotor Arm
2. Points gap
3. Cam lobes
4. Pressure pad (lubrication point)
5. Felt pad (lubrication point)
6. Cut-out in baseplate

29D. DUCELLIER DISTRIBUTORS: Very lightly smear the cam (3) with grease, lubricate the pressure pad (4) with grease and add a few drops of oil to the felt pad (5) in the top of the cam spindle.

Turn the crankshaft until the distributor centrifugal weight pivot post is visible through the cut-out in the base plate (6) and lubricate the pivot post with a drop of oil; repeat for the opposite pivot post. (Illustration, courtesy Rover Group Ltd.)

30A

30B

☐ **Job 30. Check ignition timing and dwell.**

CONTACT BREAKER IGNITION ONLY

30A. You can time the ignition sufficiently accurately to get the engine running by turning the engine till the rotor arm is pointing towards the stud in the cap for number 1 cylinder and the timing mark on the crankshaft pulley is at the appropriate mark. In this position, slacken the clamp holding the body of the distributor, rotate it till the points are just about to open, and tighten the clamp. This will not do for anything more than getting the engine running so that you can take your Metro for **SPECIALIST SERVICE**.

30B. If you want to do the job yourself, by far the most efficient method is to use a stroboscopic timing light. This device clips over the plug lead to No. 1 cylinder with two other leads to the battery. When the engine runs, a 'stroboscopic' light is triggered at the precise point in unison with the spark plug. Aiming the light at the timing marks has the effect of freezing the action long enough to check that the pully notch and timing pointer meet. To further enhance this, a little dab of white paint (typist's correction fluid works perfectly and dries immediately) on the appropriate pointer or flywheel/torque converter scale, and on the pulley notch, will make the marks even more visible. Disconnect the vacuum advance pipe at the distributor and plug the pipe end. The engine should be set to run at the correct rpm figure as shown in *Chapter 8, Facts and Figures* (most timing lights incorporate an RPM indicator) and the timing checked.

Should the timing need to be corrected, the distributor needs to be rotated to alter the point at which the contact breaker points just open. At the base of the distributor is a clamp plate with either a locknut or retaining bolt, as shown in 30A. Loosen this, not too much so that the distributor is sloppy but enough that it will move when pressure is applied. Start the engine and let it run until it settles at the correct rpm (adjust if necessary). Aim the timing light at the timing marks, turn the engine off again and rotate the distributor (the direction depends on whether the timing is out in retard or advance) then restart the engine and check again, until the timing marks align. Switch off the engine and re-tighten the clamp. Re-check the timing again in case the act of tightening the clamp has disturbed the distributor.

If you have removed the distributor you will need to reset the timing of it before you put it back. Full details for doing this are in Job 71.

SAFETY FIRST!
Don't try adjusting the distributor with the engine running!

31A

☐ **Job 31. Setting ignition dwell.**

CONTACT BREAKER IGNITION ONLY

31A. Setting the points gap with feeler gauges is accurate enough for general running but, for spot-on accuracy and best fuel consumption, the gap should be set by using a dwell meter. **SPECIALIST SERVICE**: Once again, this is a job that your specialist will do for you, or you can buy a dwell meter - DIY versions are not expensive - and learn to use it by following the instructions with the meter.

31B. To set the points gap 'manually', turn the distributor shaft till the heel of the moving point is on one of the lobes of the centre cam (29B.3). Slacken the adjusting screw (29B. 11) and, as shown here, insert a feeler gauge of the appropriate thickness (29B.2) (see *Chapter 8, Facts and Figures*). Adjust the moving point with a screwdriver (29B.10) and tighten the screw when the feeler gauge is a sliding fit between the points (see Job 71F). This will give you a points gap which is accurate enough for starting the engine but, to get the gap absolutely accurate, you need to use a dwell meter, see Job 31.

31B

☐ **Job 32. Alternator/fan belt.**

SAFETY FIRST!
Disconnect the battery before working on the drive belts so that the engine cannot be inadvertently started or turned over, causing personal injury.

32A. There are two methods of checking the tension on the drive belt for the dynamo (alternator on later models). The first is to twist it. On the top run it should twist through about 90 degrees with moderate pressure. As a second check, there should be about 1/2 inch (12 mm) movement on the longest run when deflected with moderate finger pressure as shown here. The deflection you are looking for is towards the pulley, pushing the belt into the grooves, not backwards and forwards.

32A

32B. If the belt shows any signs of fraying or cracking it should be replaced. The modern type of belt with teeth on the inside can be checked properly only by taking it off. Bend it inside out and look for signs of cracking between the teeth.

INSIDE INFORMATION: Because it is difficult to check the modern type of belt without taking it off, it is wise to carry a spare as your car will not be drivable should the belt break (the sign is the ignition warning light coming on). Make sure, too, that you carry the right size spanners to be able to change the belt, and a piece of wood to tension it. With a new belt but no tools, you are still stranded!

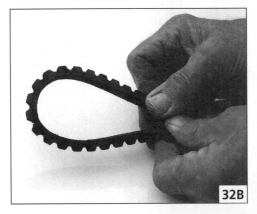
32B

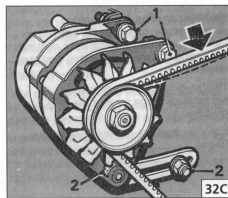
32C

32C. To adjust or remove the belt, first slacken off the mounting bolts shown here and the adjustment bolts underneath the drive pulley. (Illustration, courtesy Rover Group Ltd.)

32D. For the three bolts which pass through the alternator, you will need a spanner to hold the bolt while you undo the nut. If you are fitting a new belt, push the alternator towards the engine and feed the belt over the pulleys.

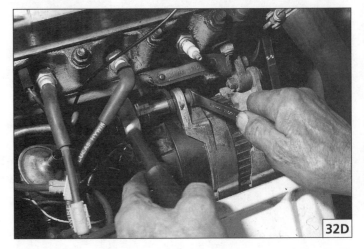
32D

3,000 MILE SERVICE

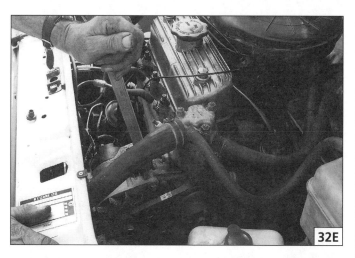

32E. Then use a piece of wood between the engine and the dynamo or alternator to lever it out till you get the correct tension on the belt. Hold this tension while you tighten the adjusting nuts.

> *making it easy!* To make adjustment easier, slacken the mounting bolts until the generator can be moved with moderate leverage on the piece of wood but not so slack that it flops down. Don't pull so hard on the lever that you damage the alternator casing! Then, put a socket spanner on the adjustment bolt that goes through the long groove in the adjustment strap, lever the generator out and check the tension. Tighten the adjustment bolt and the generator will stay in that position while you tighten the other bolts. Don't overtighten a drive belt; it shortens its life and puts unnecessary strain on the end bearing of the generator.

☐ Job 33. Check air filter.

33A. Air cleaners on non-turbocharged cars vary slightly in shape, but they are all held to the top of the carburettor with two long through-nuts with wing grips on the top.

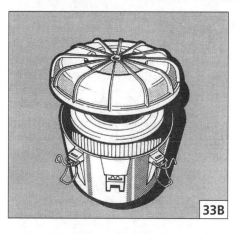

33B. On Turbo cars, the air cleaner is to the right of the alternator as you stand in front of the car. The cover is held by hand clips. (Illustration, courtesy Rover Group Ltd.)

33C. If the element shows just a slight soiling give it a light tap to remove any loose dust, and replace it with the soiled part turned to a different position.

33D. If, however, it is dirty, replace it. Dust out the cleaner bowl and make sure that the new element sits down tightly.

3,000 MILE SERVICE

33E. Check the small foam pad at the entrance to the filter bowl (non-turbo cars only). If it is torn or very dirty, renew it.

33F. Check the flexible aluminium pipe where the filter bowl sits on the air intake box (non-turbo cars only). If it is damaged, cut a new one from flexible trunking which you can buy at auto. accessory shops.

☐ **Job 34. SU carburettor.**

34. OPTIONAL: An SU carburettor can go out of tune quite often, especially when it is past its first flush of youth. If you wish to adjust it at this service, refer to Job 76 in the 6,000 mile service. You might as well top up the dashpot, now that you have gone this far! (See Job 74)

☐ **Job 35. Pipes and hoses.**

35. Check all pipes and hoses in and around the engine bay for security and leaks.

Every 3,000 mile - Under the Car

☐ **Job 36. Hand brake travel.**

SAFETY FIRST!
Don't work beneath a vehicle supported only on axle stands with someone else sitting inside trying the handbrake. It's too risky that their movements will cause the vehicle to fall off the axle stands. Make sure that you are well clear of the raised vehicle when someone is inside it. Read carefully the information at the start of this chapter on lifting and supporting the vehicle.

INSIDE THE CAR: Check the hand brake lever. It must be mounted securely and must stay firmly in the 'on' position when the button is released. Sometimes, if a hand brake slips off when pushed downwards, the ratchet and pawl mechanism is sticking and a squirt or two of releasing fluid will free them. However, it is more likely that the ratchet and pawl are worn and need replacing. Seek **SPECIALIST SERVICE** if you are in any doubt.

Pull the hand brake up. It should put the brakes on fully after three or four clicks of the ratchet. If the travel is excessive it can be adjusted, but don't adjust the handbrake cable until you have checked the adjustment of the rear brake shoes, see Job 53. The cable adjuster is behind the handbrake lever between the two front seats. With the hand brake released, turn the adjusting nut half a turn at a time until the brakes are binding at three clicks and hard on at four. Check that, when the hand brake lever is released, the wheels are free to turn without binding.

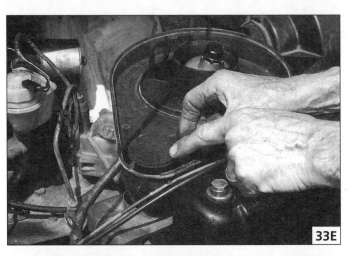
33E

33F

34

35

FACT FILE: HYDRAGAS SUSPENSION

All Metros are fitted with a highly pressurised suspension system. The positions of the valves are shown here so that you don't tamper with them in error. NEVER release the valves or disconnect any part of the system, or try to re-pressurise it yourself. For safety's sake, any work here is strictly SPECIALIST SERVICE! If the fluid pressure is lost, Rover say that it's OK to drive the car to your Dealer at up to 20 mph on normal roads. (Illustration, courtesy Rover Group Ltd.)

SAFETY FIRST!
Raise the front of the car after reading carefully the information at the start of this chapter on lifting and supporting the car.

☐ **Job 37. Steering rack gaiters.**

Check under the car that the steering rack is securely mounted to the frame and then check the condition of the gaiter at each end.

37A. Turn the steering wheel fully to the left; check the right hand steering rack gaiter for leaks and tears: squeeze and pinch the gaiter hard. Turn the steering to the right, check the left hand gaiter in the same way. As can be seen in this picture, this gaiter is split and leaking lubricant and will need to be replaced immediately.

37B. You will now have to remove the track rod end from the steering arm - see Job 38 - so that the gaiter can be replaced. Do so straight away since, without oil in the rack, its life expectancy will be very poor indeed! Take out the small nut and screw holding the retaining clip in place at each end of the old gaiter and fit the new gaiter. Some gaiters are held with metal or plastic clips which have to be cut off.

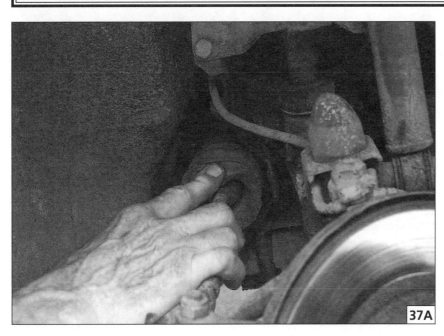

37A

37C. Using an oil can, inject fresh oil (see *Appendix 1, Recommended Castrol Lubricants*) into the gaiters to compensate for that lost (obviously the steering rack shown is one removed from the car for illustration only). You can add more later on, as the oil feeds across the rack, by removing the clip once again.

37B

37C

☐ Job 38. Track rod end gaiters.

38A. Check the rubber boot on each track rod end (TRE). If torn, renew the complete track rod end. In theory, you can replace the boot but it's a false economy for the following reasons. i) chances are that the old TRE will be worn because the boot has split and because of the resulting absence of lubricant, and ii) the TRE has to be removed from the steering arm in any case. This can be such a devil of a job to carry out that you might as well get it over with and fit a relatively inexpensive, new TRE whilst you're at it.

38B. The tapered shank system gives a very positive location but it also makes the ball joint very difficult to remove. There are ball joint removal tools (one of several types shown here) available from your local motorists' store and there is the traditional way of doing the job. With the latter, you hold one hammer against one side of the eye (on the end of the steering arm, fitted over the taper) and hit the other side sharply with a hammer. This deforms the eye enough to loosen the taper. Theoretically! In practice, you may have to use a removal tool and a pair of hammers - and to strike the eye repeatedly until a good, sharp blow shocks the joint free. You will probably cut the rubber bellows on the ball joint as you hammer, so you will have to renew it even if you are just dismantling for another job.

38C. Before you start, count the number of visible exposed threads on the steering track rod up to the nut that locks the track rod end in place (arrowed). You will have to remove this nut as well as the TRE if you're doing this job to replace a steering rack gaiter, and it's very important that the nut goes back in the same position as before. Slacken the nut, remove the other nut holding the TRE to the steering arm (knock back the lock tab first on disc brake models) then remove the TRE as just described. **SPECIALIST SERVICE:** Now have the tracking accurately re-set by your local tyre specialist.

38D. INSIDE INFORMATION: i) When you undo the self-locking nut on the old ball pin replace it with half a turn of thread to prevent the track rod jumping up into the air when the taper flies free. If, however, you put the nut back more than half a turn, you may have difficulty getting it off again as the ball pin will turn in its housing and there is nothing to grip to stop it. ii) You might find the same problem when you fit the new track rod end. If the ball pin turns in its housing when you try to tighten the self-locking nut, use a long bar hooked under the chassis rail to force the track rod end downwards so that the taper of the ball pin is gripped in the end of the steering arm. Once the nut has gone tight it will pull the taper in and you can finish tightening it without fear of the ball pin turning.

3,000 MILE SERVICE

☐ **Job 39. Drain engine oil.**

IMPORTANT NOTE: Don't forget that, on all models, the engine and transmission/gearbox share the same oil.

OPTIONAL. Some owners prefer to maximise engine life by changing the engine oil at this stage. The more usual change point is at 6,000 miles - but the choice is yours!

If you are not draining the engine oil at this service don't forget to carry out Job 1, but wait till the car is lowered to an even keel so that you do not get a false reading on the dipstick.

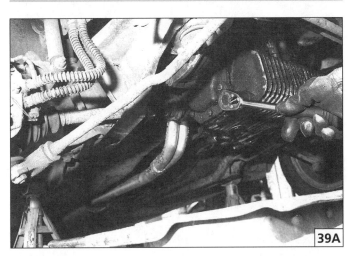

39A. Warm the engine a little before draining the oil so that the oil flows out more easily, but don't warm it so much that the oil becomes scalding hot. Running the engine until it will idle without using the choke should be sufficient.

39B. Place a container under the drain plug and protect the garage floor from drips and spillage. Draining the oil can be a messy business! Remember to replace the drain plug once the oil has drained, and use a new copper washer which you can buy from the accessory shop or garage where you bought your oil. Buy it at the same time, then you don't forget it.

39C. If your car is fitted with a drain plug having a magnet in it, clean any particles of metal from it before replacing it. You might get a shock at the amount of metal the magnet attracts, but most of it will have worn off the gear teeth and it's better on the magnet than circulating in the engine.

☐ Job 40. Change oil filter.

See IMPORTANT NOTE at the start of Job 39.

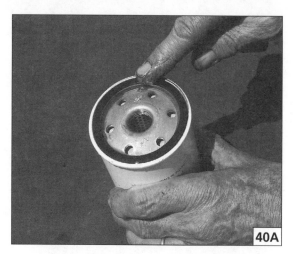

40A. On cars with manual transmission the oil filter is the familiar screw-on, throw-away thin metal cartridge type located at the front just behind the radiator. The easiest way to remove this type of filter is with a strap or chain wrench which you can buy from an accessory shop. Alternatively, though this is much more messy, you can drive a screwdriver or spike right through the cartridge and twist it off. Always put a container underneath before undoing the filter as a quantity of oil is bound to run out. Before screwing on the new filter, smear some clean engine oil round the sealing ring. Screw the filter on with firm hand pressure only. Using any type of wrench will distort it.

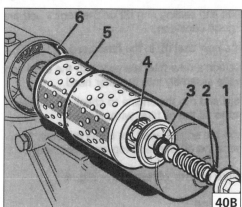

40B. Cars with automatic transmission have a different filter arrangement with a disposable cartridge inside a metal filter bowl. Place a container under the filter to catch the oil which will run out as soon as you release the bowl. You should get new seals and washers with the new element.

Unscrew the bolt to release the filter bowl and remove and throw away the element (5) and large rubber seal (6). Remove the circlip (4) and withdraw the centre bolt and its associated parts. Clean the bowl and all the parts and reassemble the centre bolt with a new sealing ring (2) and felt washer (1). Fit the new seal (6), place the new element in the filter bowl and fit the assembly into the filter head. (Illustration, courtesy Rover Group Ltd.)

☐ Job 41. Pour in fresh oil.

41. Lower the car to the ground and pour in fresh oil gradually so you do not get a sudden air lock in the rocker cover which can make the oil spurt out over the top. Dip the level occasionally, allowing time for the oil to drain down into the sump. After filling, run the engine for a few minutes to allow the oil to circulate and to fill the filter. Switch off and dip the level again, finally topping up if necessary.

☐ Job 42. Check for oil leaks.

42. After running the engine, check underneath the car, especially in the areas of the sump plug and filter, making sure that there are no oil leaks.

SAFETY FIRST!
Raise the front of the car off the ground once again, after reading carefully the information at the start of this chapter on lifting and supporting the car.

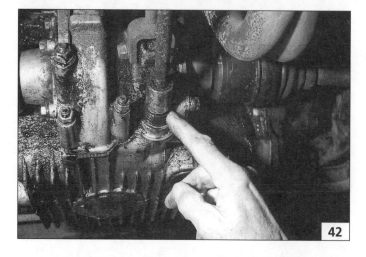

☐ Job 43. Check front brake pads.

43A

43B

43C

43A. Before you can check the condition of the front pads you have to remove the anti-rattle springs. Start by squeezing together the open ends of the two large split pins and removing them with a stout pair of pliers.

43B. After removing the split pins, lever the springs out with a screwdriver.

43C. You can check the pad thickness without going any further. The maker's recommended minimum thickness for the friction material is 3 mm (1/8 in.), but you may want to renew earlier than this because you won't be looking at the pads again for another 3,000 miles. It is normal for one pad to wear slightly more than the other but, if it appears that only one pad is doing the work and the other has hardly worn at all, it is a sign that the caliper is sticking. This means **SPECIALIST SERVICE**. Have the calipers checked by a garage.

The old pads will be quite tight against the pistons and the disc, so grip the split pin ear on the metal part of the pad with a stout pair of pliers and wriggle it to get clearance to lift it out past the slight ridge on the rim of the disc. Note that the inside pad on each front wheel has wires attached to it for the brake wear warning light. Be careful not to snap them off when you examine the pad, and undo them at the connector behind the caliper before you remove the pad. Make sure that the new pads with the wires are used in the same position.

When you look inside the calipers you will see that there are hydraulic pistons protruding from the body on each side of the disc. These are the pistons which, under hydraulic pressure from the master cylinder, force the pads against the disc to provide braking. Take a strip of rag dipped in brake fluid and clean the exposed rims of the pistons with it - like using dental floss. If the exposed part of the pistons are badly corroded, as they may be on a car which has been badly neglected, seek **SPECIALIST SERVICE**.

The pistons will have moved out of the calipers as the old discs wore down and have to be pushed back in to allow the new, thicker discs to be inserted. If the exposed part of the piston is badly corroded it could damage the hydraulic seal when it is pushed back in and lead to leaks with serious, if not fatal, consequences.

Provided the exposed parts of the pistons are clean and not corroded it's time to push them back into the calipers to make room for the new pads but, before you do this, you must make room for the hydraulic fluid which pushing them back will displace. As the old pads wore, the pistons moved out from the caliper which is why it was necessary to top up the hydraulic fluid from time to time. When the pistons are pushed back, this extra fluid has to go somewhere and, if you do not take precautions, it will flood out of the master cylinder reservoir and make a terrible mess in the engine bay.

There are different methods you can use. One is to draw some of the hydraulic fluid out of the master cylinder reservoir with a clean syringe, such as an *old* battery hydrometer. We do not recommend dipping a rag in to act as a wick-soak as there is a distinct danger of introducing dirt into the master cylinder with the chance of possible brake failure. If you use the syringe method, take care not to draw out too much fluid at a time or you could introduce air into the system and have to seek **SPECIALIST SERVICE** to have the brakes bled. Little and often is the better policy and have someone keep an eye on the reservoir while you push the pistons back to check that it does not overflow.

making it easy! An easier method of dealing with brake fluid overflow is to use a brake bleeding tube with a non-return valve at its end. You can buy these tubes in most accessory shops. Clean the brake bleed nipple it looks like a large grease nipple on the side of the caliper towards the car. Fit the end of the bleed tube over the nipple - the better tubes have a plastic clip to stop the tube coming off and put the other end, the end with the non-return valve, in a suitable container to catch the fluid. With an open ended spanner loosen the bleed nipple about half a turn. Now when you push the pistons back in, the excess fluid will run out of the bleed tube and the non-return valve will stop air being sucked back in.

The pistons will probably be too stiff to push back in by hand. Use a large woodworker's G-cramp over each side of the caliper in turn, with a thinner piece of wood against the end of the piston to get an even pull. As you tighten the clamp the piston will move back into the caliper. Once the pistons are back, and BEFORE YOU DO ANYTHING ELSE, tighten the bleed nipple again and remove the bleed tube. Never attempt to save the old brake fluid for re-use.

43F. Smear a *very* small quantity of brake grease (NOT ordinary grease!) on the backs of the pads before fitting them in position.

43G. The anti-rattle spring on Type A brakes has a bulge in it to avoid trapping the wear indicator wires. Make sure the wires pass freely under this bulge and reconnect them to the connector behind the caliper. After the pads on both sides have been replaced, tread firmly on the brake pedal several times to bring the pistons back to their normal working position and check that the brake pedal feels firm and hard. If it does not, DO NOT USE THE CAR ON THE ROAD until the problem has been resolved by a specialist.

FACT FILE: METRO BRAKE TYPES

43D. There should be a sticker on the bodywork at the front, just above the radiator, saying whether your car is fitted with Type A brakes or Type B. It is essential to know this information when you are ordering new pads. If the sticker is missing, take one of the old pads along with you and check that the new pads you buy are the correct type.

43E. The main identifying feature between the two types of pads is the spacing of the split pin holes. On Type A they are widely spaced and the top edge of the friction material is curved. On Type B they are closer together and the top edge of the friction material is straight. Also, on Type B, the anti-rattle spring is a simple cross rather than covering the whole front edge of the pads as on Type A.

43D

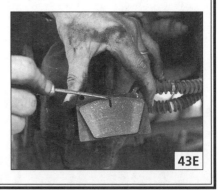

43E

43F

43G

☐ Job 44. Check front discs.

> SAFETY FIRST!
> *Brake discs which are badly ridged or worn cannot give you full braking efficiency. If you have any doubt about the condition of your discs, seek SPECIALIST SERVICE advice.*

44. While you're in the area, check both sides of the front discs visually. Unless the discs are almost new, there are bound to be slight signs of ridging on the disc surface but it must not be excessive. New pads should not be fitted to a badly ridged disc. They will give very poor braking for quite a time till the friction surface beds into the ridges and, what's more, they will not last very long. As the disc wears it develops a slight ridge or rim on the circumference because the friction surfaces of the pads do not quite reach the outside of the disc.

☐ Job 45. Check front brake hoses.

45. Check the condition of the front brake hoses. Bend them quite sharply between your finger and thumb to look for cracking of the rubber. If you find any, or if the rubber looks deteriorated in any way, seek SPECIALIST SERVICE to have them replaced.

> SAFETY FIRST!
> *See FACT FILE: HYDRAGAS SUSPENSION, before Job 37. NEVER disconnect the suspension, pipes or valves.*

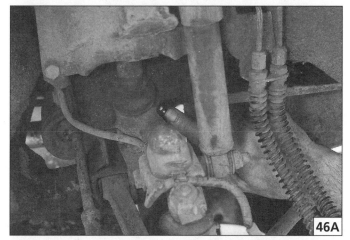

☐ Job 46. Lubricate front suspension.

46A. Lubrication of the front suspension is often neglected, but neglect here can be very costly as it is a prime cause of premature wear and MoT failure. There is a grease nipple on each side which need attention, hidden under the top suspension pivot behind the shock damper.

46B. You will need a grease gun of the lever type with a long extension to be able to reach the grease nipple on the front suspension (arrowed). Apply grease till you can see it just start to ooze from the edge of the pivot.

INSIDE INFORMATION: If you find that you cannot get grease through any of the nipples it may be that the nipple itself is blocked. Unscrew it and hold it in the vice - or a self-gripping wrench if you haven't a vice - and try pumping grease through it by itself. Hold the nipple by the hexagon flats, not the thread. If you still cannot get grease through, the nipple needs replacing. Make certain you get a new grease nipple with the correct thread as accessory shops often stock them in both metric and Imperial sizes and sometimes Unified threads as well. Forcing in a grease nipple with the wrong thread will damage the housing and make it very difficult to fit a nipple with the correct thread.

☐ Job 47. Check steering swivel boots.

47A

SAFETY FIRST!
*The Metro has ball joint steering swivels at the top and bottom of the stub axle carrier just behind the brake disc. If the rubber boots which protect these are split, allowing water and road dirt to get into the joint, the steering can become stiff and dangerous. A split boot is an MoT failure. If any of the boots are split seek **SPECIALIST SERVICE** as renewing them requires depressurising the suspension system and the use of special tools. Trying to depressurise the system at home can be very dangerous and should not be attempted.*

47A. The boot for the top steering swivel is at the end of the top suspension arm.

47B. The boot for the bottom steering swivel is at the end of the lower suspension arm, just outboard of the anti-roll bar mounting.

47B

☐ Job 48. Examine front shock absorber mountings.

48. Examine the rubber bushes at the top and bottom of the front shock absorbers. If they allow the bottom of the shock absorber to move they are well past their use-by date. If, as here, they are firm, but the edges have started to crack, keep a close eye on them and renew them before the rubber starts to break up.

☐ Job 49. Check front anti-roll bar mountings.

If any of the anti-roll bar mounting rubbers is worn, they should be replaced as a set for maximum road holding and ride comfort. Changing the anti-roll bar mounting rubbers could affect the front wheel alignment and cause rapid tyre wear so, if they have to be replaced, have the alignment checked as soon as possible afterwards.

48

49A. The outer mountings for the anti-roll bar are in the bottom suspension arm. Check that the rubber bushes are firm and not worn. The bushes cannot be replaced until the inner mounting rubbers are removed.

49B. The inner mounting rubbers for the anti-roll bar are at the front of the subframe just behind the front bumper. They are split rubber bushes which can be removed from the anti-roll bar after undoing the housing bolts.

49A

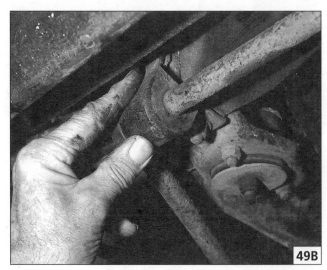

49B

☐ Job 50. Examine front suspension unit lower mounting.

The lower mounting of the front Hydragas suspension strut is a ball joint in a nylon cup and protected by a rubber boot. If this boot is split, allowing water and dirt to enter the joint, it will result in premature wear.

50. Wipe clean the rubber boot at the bottom of the Hydragas suspension strut and examine it for damage. If it is split, seek **SPECIALIST SERVICE** as renewing it means depressurising the system and the use of special tools. Trying to depressurise the system at home can be very dangerous and should not be attempted.

☐ Job 51. Examine drive shaft gaiters.

51A. Put the front wheel on full lock and, with the gear lever in neutral, turn the hub while you spread the folds of the drive shaft outer gaiter to examine it for splits.

51B. While you are under the car, get an assistant to turn each hub gently while you spread the folds of the inner gaiter and look for splits.

> **SAFETY FIRST!**
> *If you find a split in any of the four drive gaiters, have a specialist renew them at once. A split will allow water and road dirt to enter with the possibility of the joint seizing with dangerous results.*

☐ Job 52. Check front wheelnuts torque.

52. Refit the front wheels, tighten the wheel nuts reasonably tight with the wheels off the ground and tighten them fully when the wheels are back on the ground with the weight of the car on them. We strongly recommend the use of a torque wrench to check the tightness of the wheel nuts. If you do not have a suitable torque wrench, tighten the nuts and have the torques checked by a garage at the first opportunity. Wheel nut torques are important. Overtightened nuts can damage the threads or can damage alloy wheels as well as over-stressing the studs. You could also find yourself stranded by the roadside should you get a puncture and your car's wheel brace will not shift them! Nuts which are not tight enough can lead to loose wheels and (obviously!) very dangerous consequences.

INSIDE INFORMATION: When checking wheel nuts with a torque wrench, always slacken them slightly first, ensure that the nut spins freely on the thread, and then torque to the correct figure. Otherwise an under-or-over-tightened nut will not show up.

☐ Job 53. Adjust rear brakes.

Lower the front of the car to the ground, slacken the rear wheel nuts slightly and raise the rear end of the car on to axle stands. Remove the rear wheels.

> **SAFETY FIRST!**
> *Raise car off the ground only after reading carefully the information at the start of this chapter on lifting and supporting the car.*

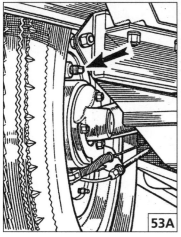

53A. The rear brake shoe adjuster is on the inside of the backplate at the top and has a small squared end to take the adjuster tool. Turn the adjuster clockwise (screwing it in to the backplate) until it goes hard and the drum is locked. Apply the footbrake hard to centralise the shoes, then back the adjuster off just enough to let the drum turn freely. The drum should turn freely after only two or three 'clicks' of the adjuster. If you need to back the adjuster off excessively, and the drum turns with a tight-free movement. You need to look further inside. See Jobs 112 and 113. (Illustration, courtesy AP Lockheed)

making it easy! The rear brake adjusters have small squared ends, and are notorious for seizing when cars get older and have been neglected. The squared ends also have a habit of rounding off where people have tried to use an ill-fitting, thin spanner to turn them instead of the proper tool. You can buy a brake adjusting tool at most accessory shops. It looks like a spanner but it is much thicker and has an open jaw at one end and a square hole at the other. Always use the square hole if you can, to get a better grip. If you cannot get the proper tool, use an adjustable wrench with thick jaws that is in good condition rather than a thin-jawed open-ended spanner.

INSIDE INFORMATION: If the squared end has rounded so much that you cannot get a grip, the adjuster needs replacing. This means stripping the brake shoes and, if you do not feel competent to do this yourself, it's SPECIALIST SERVICE time.

53B. If the adjuster is working OK, clean the threads with a wire brush and smear a layer of grease over them. This will prevent the adjuster seizing before the next 3,000 mile service. (Illustration, courtesy AP Lockheed)

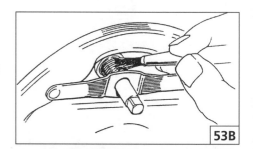
53B

☐ Job 54. Check rear brake pipes.

54. Check the condition of the brake pipes which run along the suspension arms from the flexible hoses to the rear brakes. Light surface rust is acceptable but, if any of the pipes are rusty, as this one certainly is, seek SPECIALIST SERVICE to have the rusty pipe or pipes renewed.

54

☐ Job 55. Check rear flexible hoses.

55. Examine the rear flexible hoses for signs of cracking or ageing. They are not long enough to be bent very much, the normal way to disclose cracks, so don't skimp this inspection. If you are in doubt about their condition, seek SPECIALIST ADVICE.

☐ Job 56. Check rear suspension.

SAFETY FIRST!
Note the FACT FILE before Job 37. NEVER disconnect the suspension pipes or valves.

55

56A. Check the pipes which carry the fluid to and from the Hydragas suspension units. As with brake pipes, light surface rust is acceptable but, if they are deeply pitted with rust, seek **SPECIALIST SERVICE** to have them replaced. Check that the large rubber bump stops, mounted above the rear suspension arm, are secure and in good condition. If they are damaged, or missing, replace them. They are held only by a single bolt, though you may find that the nut has rusted tight.

TURBO MODELS ONLY

56B. Check all four rubber bushes (and for corrosion in the body mounting brackets) of the rear anti-roll bar. Replace rubber bushes if they appear soft or spreading. (Illustration, courtesy Rover Group Ltd.)

56A

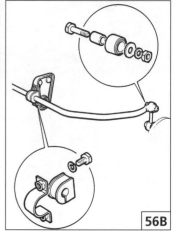
56B

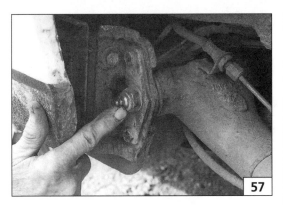

Job 57. Lubricate rear suspension.

57. There is a grease nipple each side of the car at the ends of the suspension arm pivots. They are often neglected, but neglect here can be very costly in terms of suspension arm replacements.

making it easy! If you find that you cannot get grease through any of the nipples it may be that the nipple itself is blocked. Unscrew it and hold it in the vice - or a self-gripping wrench if you haven't a vice - and try pumping grease through it by itself. Hold the nipple by the hexagon flats, not the thread.

INSIDE INFORMATION: If you still cannot get grease through, the nipple needs replacing. Make certain you get a new grease nipple with the correct thread as accessory shops often stock them in both metric and Imperial sizes and sometimes Unified threads as well. Forcing in a grease nipple with the wrong thread will damage the housing and make it very difficult to fit a nipple with the correct thread.

Job 58. Check rear wheel nuts torque.

Refit the rear wheels, tighten the wheel nuts reasonably tight with the wheels off the ground and tighten them fully when the wheels are back on the ground with the weight of the car on them. See Job 52 for details.

SAFETY FIRST!
Raise the car off the ground only after reading carefully the information at the start of this chapter on lifting and supporting the car. Wear goggles when carrying out any cleaning, painting or undersealing underneath the car.

Job 59. Inspect underside.

First, clean off the underside of your car. When the underside of the car is dry, inspect it for rust and damage to the underbody sealant. Look particularly for loose, flaking sealant and, if necessary, scrape it off with a flat bladed paint scraper. If you expose the metal, treat the area with rust killer, then a good quality paint and finally a new coat of sealant. While you are doing this you may also find small jobs to do like renewing clips for wiring, pipe runs and so on, and check particularly the brake pipes for corrosion. If the surface of the pipes look pitted and rough, seek SPECIALIST SERVICE and have the corroded pipes replaced with copper or cupro-nickel non-corroding pipes.

Every 3,000 miles - Around the Car

Job 60. Wiper blades and arms.

Run a few drops of oil on to the spindles of the wipers and check the operation and the 'sweep' of the arms. NOTE! Always wet the screen before running the wiper blades over it. Even a small amount of dust or grit can scratch the glass. If the sweep is wrong it can be altered by moving the wiper arms on the spindle splines. The method of fixing the arms varies. Sometimes there is a small screw to undo and on others there is a small catch, which you lift with a screwdriver after folding the arm back away from the screen. Make sure that the catch is engaged properly, or the fixing screw is tight, after adjustment.

Job 61. Check windscreen.

Check the windscreen for scratches, cracks, chips or other damage. See *Chapter 7, Getting Through the MoT,* for what is and what isn't acceptable under UK regulations.

INSIDE INFORMATION: Small stone chips, cracks and scratches on a windscreen can often be repaired nowadays by windscreen specialists. If you find any damage, seek SPECIALIST SERVICE as soon as possible. The longer you delay the more likely it is that weather will get in the crack or chip and make the repair more difficult. Early treatment could save you the cost of an expensive screen.

Job 62. Check floors.

62. Lift the carpets and check for signs of rust or water on the floor underneath. If you find any, deal with it before any leaks are left for so long that you face the problem of seriously rusted metal as well. If you find any wetness, you will probably have to take the seats and the carpets right out to dry the carpets and any underfelt. Tracing leaks isn't the easiest of jobs, and sometimes the only way

is to dry the floor thoroughly and then get someone play a hose on the underside of the car, round the doors and over the bonnet while you look inside.

Every 3,000 mile - Road Test

☐ **Job 63. Clean controls.**

The door handles, steering wheel, switches and gear lever knob may well have become greasy from handling while you were carrying out the service. Clean them with a rag moistened with hot water containing a little detergent.

☐ **Job 64. Check instruments and controls.**

64. Switch on the ignition while sitting in the driving seat and check that all the warning lights which should come, do come on. Warning lights which do not work are useless as warnings! Non-functioning may be just a case of a blown bulb, but it may be a symptom of deeper electrical trouble. If changing a bulb does not cure the problem, or if the warning lights fail to go out when they should, seek **SPECIALIST SERVICE** from an auto electrician. Check that all the switches are secure and working.

☐ **Job 65. Throttle and choke cables.**

65. Operate the throttle pedal several times to check that it is smooth over its complete travel. A throttle pedal which is stiff or, worse still, which sticks, can be dangerous as well as making driving a misery. Check the smoothness of operation of the choke. If either is not as smooth as it should be, check the route of the cables to make sure there are no sharp bends or kinks and check that the inner cables are not fraying where it comes out of the outer casing. Later throttle cables with a nylon inner sleeve are much smoother in operation that the older steel sleeve sort. If the fault for a jerky or stiff throttle pedal or choke knob is not the cable, check the linkage at the carburettor for stiffness and lubricate if necessary.

☐ **Job 66. Road Test of brakes and steering.**

Only a proper brake tester at an MoT testing station can check the operation of the brakes accurately enough for the MoT test, but you can rule out some of the most obvious braking problems on a short road test in the following way. Always check the brakes at low speed first, before attempting to brake from higher speeds. Drive at about 20 mph, dip the clutch and, with your hands only lightly gripping the wheel, try braking first gently, then harder, though there is no need to do an 'emergency' stop. Ideally, the car should pull up in a perfectly straight line. If the steering wheel kicks in your fingers, if there are any 'clonks' or other noises from underneath, if the car drifts heavily to one side as you brake, or if the brake pedal does not feel firm in operation, drive home very slowly and carefully to investigate further.

> **SAFETY FIRST!**
> *Carry out the these tests only in daylight, in clear, dry conditions ensure that all tools and equipment are removed from under and around the car and, particularly, under the bonnet. Choose a quiet road when there are no other road users or pedestrians about. Use your mirrors to make sure there are no other vehicles following you before carrying out brake tests.*

If all seems well, repeat the braking tests from a higher speed, say about 40 mph. Again, the car should, ideally, pull up in a straight line. If it drifts just gently to the left when you are on the nearside of the road, this may be due to road camber. Try to repeat the test on a non-cambered stretch of road or find a one-way street where you can try on the other side of the road to see if opposite camber has the same effect.

Check that the steering feels positive, does not kick back unduly over rough surfaces and that the car runs in a straight line when you are holding the steering wheel only lightly. Again, slight drifting may be due to road camber, but more persistent drifting needs investigating. Check that the steering self-centres when accelerating out of both left and right hand turns and, if you can find a suitably deserted stretch of road, pull the car from side to side to see that it straightens itself up. This check can be carried out at quite low speed, 15 to 20 mph is sufficient to show up any faults.

Braking and steering are a vital part of a car's safety. If you find any faults, or even if you are uneasy about anything, seek **SPECIALIST SERVICE** before you carry on using the car.

Every 6,000 Miles - or Every Six Months, Whichever Comes First

Every 6,000 miles - The Engine Bay

All of the Engine Bay Jobs in this section are carried out with the engine cold, partly for safety reasons - the risks involved in possible fuel spillage when changing the fuel filter near hot components - and partly for comfort and ease of working.

☐ **Job 67. Cooling system.**

> **SAFETY FIRST!**
> *Work on the cooling system only when the engine, and thus the coolant - is cold. When it is hot, the system is under pressure and you could get a nasty scald if you remove any caps or undo any hoses.*

67A. Check the cooling system for leaks and all hoses for tightness and condition.

INSIDE INFORMATION: Squeeze the large radiator hoses. If they go soft and soggy under your fingers the walls have started to collapse. Listen also for any cracking sounds which indicate that the hose is so old it has hardened and could give way. A hose which bursts always bursts in the most awkward possible place, so change any suspect ones now. Pay particular attention to the heater hoses - they are often neglected.

making it easy! When you buy a new hose you may find it very tight and difficult to get on to the radiator or engine connection. Sometimes even the correct size hose seems too small. A useful tip is to smear the inside lightly with waterproof grease and then use a tapered glass bottle - like an orange squash bottle - as a mandrel to open the end of the hose slightly before fitting it.

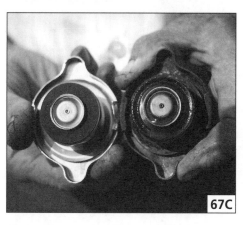

67B. Remove the expansion tank filler cap and examine the sealing washer.

67C. INSIDE INFORMATION: Look at the difference between a worn-out washer and a new one. A worn washer will allow pressure to escape and coolant to your engine may 'boil over' because, at a lower pressure, the coolant boils at a lower temperature. If yours is worn, buy a complete new cap.

67D. Make sure you buy a cap with the correct poundage spring. Your supplier will know the correct one for your model, and the poundage will be shown on the top of the cap.

☐ Job 68. Check coolant.

68.   An only satisfactory way to check the strength of the antifreeze in your coolant is to use a hydrometer, similar to the one used to check a battery but with a different scale. The float inside will indicate the strength of the antifreeze and, if it is too low, top up with neat antifreeze, replace the cap and run the engine for just a moment or two to circulate it but not enough for the coolant to get hot, then check the reading again. Don't take chances and guess that the antifreeze is strong enough, a ruined radiator - or even engine - is a high price to pay for not taking a little extra trouble.

INSIDE INFORMATION: Be very careful about spilling antifreeze, it will strip your paintwork as effectively as any paint stripper even though it takes longer. Should you spill any, even diluted in the coolant, wash it off with plenty of cold water at once.

☐ Job 69. Check water pump.

Check the water pump for leaks. It isn't always easy to spot leaks here, but look for tell-tale signs of coolant staining on the timing chain cover, on the right of the engine as you stand in front facing the car.

☐ Job 70. Fit new spark plugs.

OPTIONAL: Fit new spark plugs after checking that the gaps are correct. Some owners feel it is unnecessary to change a spark plug that seems in good condition and workng perfectly, but plugs fall off gradually in performance with age so you may not notice the deterioration in engine performance and economy. In any case, don't run plugs longer than 12,000 miles.

☐ Job 71. Renew contact breaker points and capacitor.

CARS WITHOUT ELECTRONIC IGNITION ONLY

> *SAFETY FIRST!*
> **You may minimise the risk of shock when the engine is running by wearing thick rubber gloves and by NEVER working on the system in damp weather or when standing on damp ground. Read Chapter 1 Safety First! before carrying out any work on the ignition system.**

Two makes of contact breaker distributor are fitted to the Metro: Lucas and Ducellier. They are easily identified because the Ducellier version has its tubular capacitor on the outside, the fixed and moving points are separate and the moving point is held by a wire clip whereas, on the Lucas distributor, the capacitor is inside the distributor and the fixed and moving points are made as an assembly. We will deal first with the Lucas version.

making it easy! *The distributor is at the front of the engine low down behind the radiator which makes replacement of the points and capacitor a very awkward job. We strongly recommend that you remove the distributor and take it to the bench for this job. Remove the distributor cap, disconnect the vacuum advance and retard pipe from the distributor, slacken the clamp bolt holding the distributor to the engine and lift the distributor out. The bottom of the shaft is offset which means that it can go back only one way so, provided you do not turn the engine over while the distributor is out, you will not upset the ignition timing.*

71A. To remove the points assembly, first take out the screw holding the fixed point to the baseplate.

68

71A

FACT FILE: CB POINTS AND CAPACITOR

Like spark plugs, the efficiency of contact breaker points falls off gradually in normal use so that you get a fluffy rather than a sharp break in the low tension current. This means that the coil cannot deliver its full voltage to the plugs so you get a fall off in engine performance. You can't see any fall off in performance of a capacitor by examining it but, like other electrical components, the efficiency does deteriorate, shortening the life of the points. Both points and capacitors are so cheap that it is false economy to try to extend their life.

71B

71C

71B. Then lift the complete points assembly up from the distributor.

71C. Push lightly on the spring and unhook the brass terminal from the hook in the end of the spring.

71D. Feed the black low-tension cable through the side of the distributor and remove the cross headed screw holding the capacitor.

71E. Now you can lift the capacitor and cables away from the distributor. When you buy new ones ensure that you get the capacitor complete with both cables. When you fit it, note that there is an internal wire, covered in a black fabric sleeve, that fits under the capacitor and is held by the same screw.

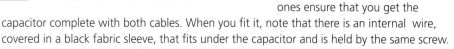

71D

71F. After feeding the black low-tension lead through the distributor, hook the brass terminal back on the points assembly, fit the points and lightly tighten the screw just enough to stop the fixed point sliding. Turn the centre shaft of the distributor till the heel of the moving point is on one of the four lobes of the centre cam. Slacken the screw holding the fixed point and adjust it till the correct feeler gauge - see *Chapter 8, Facts and Figures* - will just slide between the two points. Tighten, but don't over-tighten the screw holding the fixed point. Test the gap with the heel of the moving point on the other three lobes of the cam. If you get a wide variation in the gaps, it means that the bearings of the distributor centre shaft are worn. The car will still run if you set the points on the cam lobe which gives the smallest gap but, for best efficiency, the distributor should be replaced. Setting the gap with a feeler gauge is accurate enough to get the engine running but, for the best performance and economy, the gap should be tested and set using a dwell meter.

See Job 31.

71F

71E

71G. If the end of the brass part of the rotor arm is just lightly burnt you can clean it with fine glasspaper. If it is badly burnt, get a new one.

71H. Give the distributor cap a good clean before you replace it and check carefully inside for any signs of tracking. This shows as a burnt line between two of the brass studs. If you find any, the cap is not fit for further service. It will let you down and needs replacing.

71I. The drive dog on the distributor shaft is offset so, provided you have not turned the engine with the distributor out, the timing will be in the same position as it was. However, it needs checking.

71G

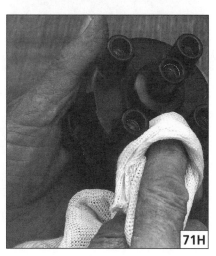

71H

71I

71J. The Ducellier distributor is, in some ways, easier to deal with than the Lucas, but slightly more fiddling in others. Changing the capacitor is simpler as it is on the outside of the distributor body. The cable from it just plugs into the supply block on the side of the distributor and the body of the capacitor is held by a single screw.

The contact points are separate, so there are two parts to remove and replace. To change the points, remove the spring clip from the pivot posts, remove the fibre washer and lift the moving contact off its post. Lift the low tension supply block out of the distributor body complete with the moving point. Remove the screw and washer and lift the fixed contact off the baseplate. Fitting a new set of points and a new capacitor is a simple reversal of taking the old ones out. In other respects, servicing it is similar to servicing the Lucas distributor. (Illustration, courtesy Rover Group Ltd.)

SPECIALIST SERVICE: We strongly recommend that, after servicing the Ducellier unit, you take the car to your dealer for them to check the dwell and the vacuum advance as the latter requires a special tool and a vacuum pump.

INSIDE INFORMATION: New points are covered with a protective film of grease which has to be cleaned off the points faces. Use a rag moistened in methylated spirit. Before fitting the new points, dribble a few drops of oil down inside the distributor base plate to lubricate the mechanical advance and retard mechanism, put a few drops of oil on the felt pad where the rotor arm fits and smear just a trace of high melting point grease on the four lobes of the distributor cam. Take care not to get grease on the faces of the points. For some reason, many people seem to think that the screw holding the fixed point has to be forced home very tight with a large screwdriver. You often find screws on which the slot in the head has been mauled. If this is the case with your car, get a new screw when you buy the new points, you do not get a new one with the points set.

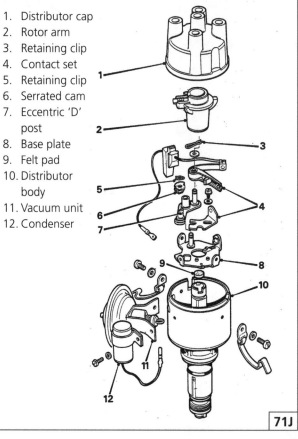

1. Distributor cap
2. Rotor arm
3. Retaining clip
4. Contact set
5. Retaining clip
6. Serrated cam
7. Eccentric 'D' post
8. Base plate
9. Felt pad
10. Distributor body
11. Vacuum unit
12. Condenser

71J

CARS WITH ELECTRONIC IGNITION ONLY

SAFETY FIRST!
THE ELECTRONIC IGNITION SYSTEM INVOLVES VERY HIGH VOLTAGES! All manufacturers recommend that only trained personnel should go near the high-tension circuit (coil, distributor and HT wiring) and it is ESSENTIAL that anyone wearing a medical pacemaker device does not go near the ignition system. Also, stroboscopic timing requires the engine to be running - take great care that parts of the timing light or parts of you don't get caught up in the moving parts! Don't wear loose clothing or hair.

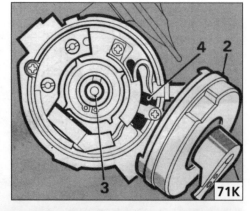

71K

71K. The distributor for electronic ignition is not serviceable at home except for lubrication. Lift off the rotor arm (1) and the plastic dust shield (2), and apply a few drops of oil to the top of the rotor shaft (3) plus a few drops through the gap (4) in the baseplate to lubricate the centrifugal weights mechanism. (Illustration, courtesy Rover Group Ltd.)

☐ Job 72. Ignition timing.

72. Replace the distributor in the engine and turn the rotor arm till the drive dog engages and you can push the distributor fully home. Tighten the clamp bolt lightly, remove the distributor cap and turn the engine till the rotor arm is pointing towards, the stud in the cap which feeds number 1 sparking plug and the contact points are just opening.

72

Sometimes, this position is not easy to determine. It helps if you connect a lamp and battery (any low voltage will do) between the low tension lead - the one you renewed with the capacitor - and engine earth. The lamp will light when the points are closed and, as you turn the engine, the position when the points just open is indicated by the lamp going out.

Now look at the front crankshaft pulley where you will see a notch in the rim and behind this, on the timing cover, a serrated pointer. This pointer has one large tooth and several small ones. The large tooth indicates Top Dead Centre (TDC). Each successive small tooth indicates an increment of 4 degrees before TDC. The static timing for a Metro is 4 degrees before TDC, so the notch ought to be opposite the small tooth next to the next large one. If it is not, turn the engine till it is and return to the distributor. Without turning the engine, slacken the distributor clamp bolt and rotate the distributor slightly till the test lamp just goes out. Tighten the clamp bolt after adjustment.

making it easy! When checking the distributor advance, sucking on the advance and retard pipe with your mouth is not often very efficient, nor pleasant, but you can make an efficient tester by reversing the washer in an ordinary bicycle pump so that it sucks instead of pumps. Attach the flexible connector on the end of the pump to the advance and retard pipe on the distributor and gently draw the pump handle back. As you do so, you should see the baseplate carrying the contact breaker move. Don't jerk the pump handle back hard or you could create enough suction to split the diaphragm in the distributor.

Static timing is sufficiently accurate to get the engine started and running but, for maximum efficiency and economy, the timing should be checked dynamically with a strobe lamp. You can either buy a strobe lamp at an accessory shop and follow the instructions or get a garage to check it for you. See Job 30.

INSIDE INFORMATION: The size of the points gap affects the timing so always set the points gap before timing the ignition. Use a dwell meter to set the gap accurately before using a strobe lamp. If you buy a strobe lamp, get one with a Xenon light. The cheaper ones with a neon light work all right but the light is difficult to see in bright daylight and almost impossible to see in sunlight. It helps to see the timing marks if you rub a piece of chalk over them first.

When you have the distributor on the bench, you can check that the vacuum advance and retard is working.

IMPORTANT NOTE: Some cars have a transmission controlled spark advance system consisting of a solenoid operated valve in the vacuum line between the inlet manifold and the vacuum mechanism on the distributor. The solenoid is controlled by an inhibitor switch mounted under the car behind the gear change remote control housing. This limits operation of the advance system to fourth gear only. With the solenoid NOT energised, the vacuum line to the distributor is vented to atmosphere and the line to the manifold is sealed. When fourth gear is selected, the solenoid is energised and vacuum is applied to the distributor advance capsule.

INSIDE INFORMATION: To check the operation, apply the handbrake and chock the front wheels. Increase the engine idle speed to 2,500 rpm, tread on the clutch pedal and hold fourth gear with the clutch disengaged. If the system is working, the engine speed will increase by 300 to 400 rpm. If it does not, the fault could mean just a simple adjustment of the inhibitor switch, but it could be the switch itself, the solenoid or a circuit fault, so seek SPECIALIST SERVICE.

Job 73. Fuel connections.

Check the fuel line connections from the pump to the carburettors to make sure there are no leaks and that the pipes are not chafing. Note: to show any leaks, the engine must be running to pressurise the system. Follow the **SAFETY FIRST!** rule of keeping tools, cloths, clothing and fingers away from the water pump drive belt and thermostatic fan.

☐ **Job 74. Top up carburettor dashpot.**

NON-TURBO CARS ONLY

74A. Remove the air cleaner, unscrew the dashpot cap on the SU carburettor and lift out the plunger. This plunger is a damper to stop the piston and needle in the carburettor fluttering and to hold the piston steady on hard accelera-

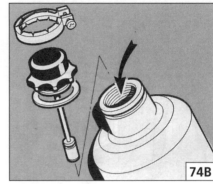

tion. If they are dry you will get poor pick-up and poor acceleration. Top the dashpot up with engine oil or general lubricating oil to the top of the hollow stem of the piston.

TURBO CARS ONLY

74B. SAFETY FIRST! On Turbo cars, remove the clamp before taking out the dashpot plunger and remember to replace it afterwards. Do NOT run the car without this clamp in place. (Illustration, courtesy Rover Group Ltd.)

☐ **Job 75. Overhaul carburettor.**

NON-TURBO CARS ONLY

SAFETY FIRST!
Read carefully the information in Chapter 1, Safety First! especially that regarding the safety hazards surrounding petrol (gasoline). In addition, note that you will have to run the engine with the air cleaners removed. There is a very slight risk of carburettor flashback, so don't get your face or your clothing too close. Also, have a workshop-sized fire extinguisher handy and make sure it is a type which can be used on petrol fires. If a fire should break out, turn off the ignition immediately to stop the engine and fuel pump and prevent any more petrol being pumped through. Because of the fire risk, and because of the very real danger of exhaust fumes, carry out the next part of this work out of doors.

Many owners fight shy of checking over an SU carburettor but, if your engine is not running well, the job can be done at home with the simplest of tools and a little care, saving you a great deal of money. What is essential is that the sparking plugs, contact breaker points, ignition timing and valve clearances are all set correctly. You should by now have dealt with the ignition jobs, but if your tappets are clattery, attend to Job 102 to set the clearances correctly before carrying out this work.

To make the photographs clearer, we have taken the carburettor off the engine to illustrate these jobs but normally they would be carried out with the carburettor in place. (On the Metro, the carburettor is difficult to see and to photograph!)

75A. As a preliminary, check for wear in the throttle spindle by trying to rock it.

INSIDE INFORMATION: There is a lot of uninformed talk about wear at the throttle spindle. Serious wear will affect the efficiency of the carburettor all the time, but slight wear will allow air leaks only at tick-over when the depression at the throttle spindles is high. Once past fast tick-over, slight wear at the spindles will have no measurable effect. Only consider overhauling the carb. (for this reason) if the wear is severe.

75B. The first job in setting the carburettor is to ensure that the piston is free in the carburettor dashpot. Remove the air cleaner, put your finger down inside air intake, lift the carburettor piston in and let it drop. It should fall smoothly and stop at the bottom with a slight 'clunk'. If it sticks or hesitates, you need to take the dashpot off for cleaning.

75C

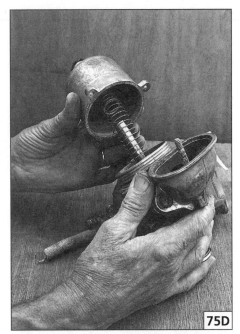

75D

75C. There are three screws holding the dashpot, and these three screws are offset so that the dashpot can be fitted in one position only, so there is no need to mark it before taking it off.

75D. Lift the dashpot up slowly after removing the screws. Inside you will find the piston and a long, whippy coiled spring. If you are not careful, this will bounce off in to the engine and, if it gets distorted, you will need a new one.

75E. Lift the piston out of the carburettor taking care not to bend the tapered brass needle at its base.

75F. Pistons usually stick in the dashpots because they need cleaning. Use only petrol or methylated spirit (industrial alcohol) to clean the grooved ring and body of the piston. Don't use anything abrasive, even as mild as metal polish. Be careful not to bend the needle while you are cleaning and testing the piston drop (see 75B). Slight movement of the needle is quite in order as it is spring loaded so that it is 'floating'.

75E

75F

75G. Clean the inside of the dashpot again using only petrol or methylated spirit, nothing abrasive. When you have cleaned the piston and dashpot thoroughly you can check it by timing the piston drop. Plug the two large air transfer holes in the base of the piston with something like Plasticine, hold the dashpot upside down, put the piston in and put a nut, bolt and washer through one of the dashpot holes. Lift the piston till it touches the washer and let it drop. It should drop easily and smoothly, and should take between five and seven seconds. Remember to remove the Plasticine plugs afterwards.

75H. If, by any mishap, you damage the needle, don't try to straighten it, fit a new one. Your Rover dealer will tell you the correct one for your model Metro. The needle is held in the piston by a clamp screw at the side, and should be fitted so that the shoulder on the needle is flush with the large base of the piston.

75G

75H

75I. On some carburettors, the guide for the piston is held by a small screw. There is no need to remove it, but satisfy yourself that the screw is tight. Should the small guide and screw come loose and drop into the engine it could cause a great deal of damage.

VERY EARLY METROS ONLY

75J. Also, while you have the dashpot off, check that the spring-loaded piston lifting pin (if fitted) is free. You could use this pin later for checking the idling mixture.

75K. The only other part of the carburettor you are likely to need to replace is the float needle valve. If there were any signs of the carburettor flooding, with petrol dripping from it, it means that the valve is not seating properly and needs replacing. To get at it you take the top off the float chamber, but be careful not to lose the small aluminium tag under one of the screws. It identifies your carburettor and you will need the figures on it if you buy new parts.

75L. On the underside of the float chamber lid you will find the tapered plastic float. Remove its hinge pin with a pair of pliers it is a fairly tight push fit - and lift the float off.

75M. With the float removed you can lift the needle valve out of its seating. The seating screws into the float chamber lid and, when you buy a new needle valve you should get a new seating with it.

75N. You will also need a new gasket for the float chamber lid as the old one is bound to be damaged getting the lid off.

IMPORTANT NOTE: When refitting the carburettor, *always* use new paper gaskets (without gasket sealer), ensuring that all mating forces are scrupulously clean before refitting the carb.

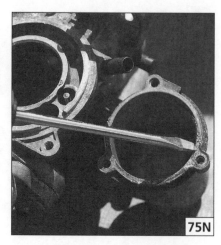

76A

76B

☐ **Job 76. Setting the carburettor.**

76A. There are three settings for the carburettor. The first is the slow-running, or idling speed. To get to this adjustment you have to prise out a tamperproof plug just alongside the dashpot to get at the slow-running adjustment screw.

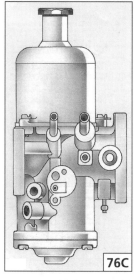

76C

76B. The second setting is the fast idle screw which is on the throttle lever and bears on the cam attached to the choke lever.

76C. The third setting is the mixture which, on the Metro, is usually a screw in the side of the carburettor under a tamperproof plug. (Illustration, courtesy Gunson)

76D. Bring the engine up to operating temperature and adjust the slow running till the engine is ticking over at the lowest speed at which it will run smoothly. Then turn the mixture screw slightly each way to see if the engine speeds up. If it does, slow it down again on the slow running throttle screw and continue till you get a smooth, even tick over.

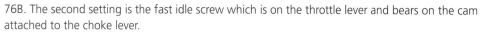

SAFETY FIRST!
Carburettor adjustment has to be carried out with a warm, running engine. Therefore: i) watch out for rotating cooling fan and drive belt, do not wear loose clothing or jewellery and tie back long hair. Remember that thermostatically controlled fans can start up without warning. ii) Take care that you do not burn yourself on the hot engine parts and/or exhaust manifolds. iii) DO NOT perform this check in your garage or any confined space - exhaust gases are highly poisonous and can kill within minutes! iv) Apply a strict No Smoking! rule whenever you are servicing your fuel system. Remember, it's not just the petrol that's flammable, it's the fumes as well. Overall, if you're not (justifiably) confident, give the job to someone who is fully competent. Some manufacturers recommend that only trained mechanics should carry out work on a vehicle's fuel system. Read Chapter 1, Safety First!

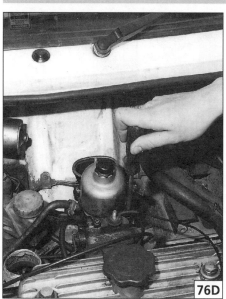

76D

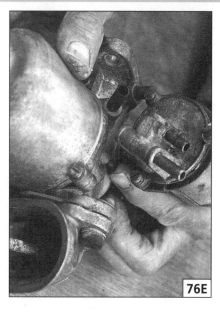

76E

VERY EARLY METROS ONLY

76E. If a piston lifting pin is fitted, push upwards lightly on the piston lifting pin to raise the piston about a sixteenth of an inch. If the engine speed stays the same, the mixture is about right. If it speeds up, the mixture is too weak, and if the engine slows down or stops, the mixture is too rich - turn the mixture screw one way or the other, if necessary to adjust the mixture. Rev the engine after each adjustment to clear the intake manifold and rest the slow running screw if necessary. Carry on until slightly lifting the pin makes no difference to the engine speed.

If you are using Gunson's Colortune plugs, or their exhaust gas analyser it makes the job more certain. In that case you adjust the mixture screw to obtain the correct reading.

INSIDE INFORMATION: It's possible that you may have a car with an early carburettor which had no mixture adjusting screw. Instead, the mixture is adjusted by raising or lowering the large brass jet nut under the main body of the carburettor. In that case, turning this nut alters the mixture, but make adjustments only one-sixth of a turn (one flat of the nut) at a time.

76F

Lastly, screw in the fast idle adjustment screw so that the engine is running at a fast tick over with the choke knob pulled out. The fast idle speed is given in *Chapter 8, Facts and Figures*, but unless you have a hand-held tachometer you will have to estimate it. Make sure that, when the choke knob is pushed in, the engine speed returns to the slow running setting.

76F. After the carburettor is set, you have to set the throttle damper. At the end of the throttle spindle on the carburettor, on the left as you stand in front of the engine, is a lever held by a pinch bolt. Slacken this pinch bolt and place a feeler gauge 0.12 in. (3 mm) thick between the end of the lever and the damper beneath it. Push down on the lever, making sure the throttle spindle does not turn, until the damper is fully compressed, then tighten the pinch bolt.

77

Refit the air cleaner after setting up and adjusting the carburettor.

☐ Job 77. Exhaust emissions.

You'll be able to set the carburettor sufficiently well for the car to run efficiently by following Job 76, but if you want to be sure of passing the MoT, it's **SPECIALIST SERVICE**. If you haven't got access to a DIY exhaust gas analyser, you will have to have a properly equipped garage such as an MoT test station, carry out an exhaust emissions check - although you'll be close by using a Colortune. Note the comments in *Chapter 7, Getting Through the MoT*, regarding the difficulty of getting SU carburettors through the MoT emissions test.

Every 6,000 miles - Around the Car

☐ Job 78. Adjust headlights.

SPECIALIST SERVICE: You can adjust your own headlights up to a point, (see Job 12), but not with sufficient accuracy to avoid dazzling other road users and, at the same time, give you the best lighting of the road. For this job, take the car to a properly equipped garage, such as an MoT test station, for them to adjust the beams with a beam setter.

80

☐ Job 79. Front wheel alignment (tracking).

SPECIALIST SERVICE: The front wheels can go out of alignment in general use, particularly if you hit pot holes in the road or bump the kerb. Specialist aligning equipment is needed to check and reset it, so you cannot do this job at home. If the alignment is not correct, the steering will be less precise and the front tyres will wear out very quickly.

☐ Job 80. Front and rear ride heights.

81

80. With the car on level ground and the tyres correctly inflated, measure the distance on each side of the car between the centre of the hub and the underside of the wheel arch. The measurements should be almost the same each side and agree with the figures given in *Chapter 8, Facts and Figures*. If there is a large discrepancy, either from the figures given, or from side to side, the Hydragas suspension system needs resetting. Seek **SPECIALIST SERVICE** - you must not attempt to work on the pressurise suspension at home. See **FACT FILE: HYDRAGAS SUSPENSION** before Job 37.

☐ Job 81. Fuel filler cap.

81. Check that the sealing ring on the fuel filler cap is in good condition. A faulty seal is an MoT failure!

OIL CHANGING - SPECIAL NOTE

Most owners prefer to change engine oil at the 6,000 mile interval, but for those who prefer a more frequent oil change schedule, we've included it under the 3,000 mile schedule as an OPTIONAL set of Jobs. See Job Number 39 to 42 for complete oil changing information. Note that you should not overfill the engine (1). The filler cap (2) is also a service replacement item see Job 99. The engine and the gearbox share the same oil and the oil is drained through a drain plug in the bottom of the gearbox, (3) being the manual type: (4) the automatic type.

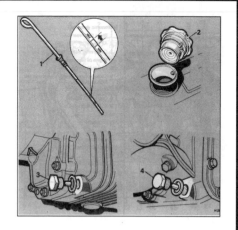

Job 82. Change alarm remote batteries.

If you have an alarm with a remote sensor, change the batteries every 6 months. Otherwise, getting in to your own car could be an alarming experience!

83A

Job 83. Lubricate bonnet release.

83A. Smear the jaws of the bonnet catch liberally with grease and put a large blob of grease on the end of the inner cable where it comes out of the outer casing to prevent water creeping down. As this catch is largely hidden under the front of the body, it pays to undo the two bolts and lift it out to carry out the greasing. Check that the bonnet closes and locks securely when you replace it. If the bonnet was to open while you are driving it could cause a nasty accident - and wouldn't do much for the bonnet!

83B. Smear a small amount of grease over the spring loaded plunger which engages with the bonnet catch.

83C. Apply some oil to the hinge of the bonnet safety catch and check that the spring loading of the catch is free and working.

Job 84. Bonnet stay.

Also, check that the bonnet stay is secure and fits properly into the front underside of the bonnet. A stay which collapses when you have your head under the bonnet can also cause a nasty accident!

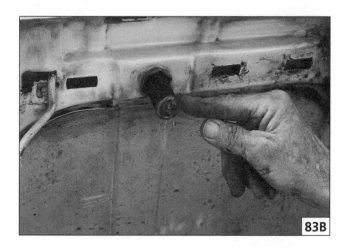

83B

83C

6,000 MILE SERVICE

☐ **Job 85.**
Lubricate locks
and hinges.

85A. Lubricate the
door and tailgate
lock mechanisms.

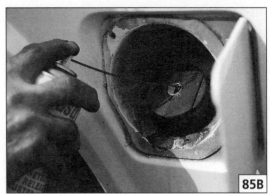

85B. Don't forget the fuel filler cap lock (when appropriate). It's embar-
rassing to say the least, if it seizes!

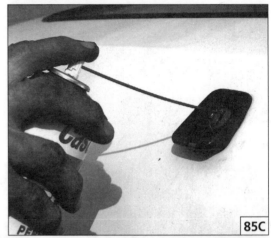

85C. Squirt a small amount of oil in the key holes to prevent the tumblers
seizing.

85D. Lubricate the door and boot
hinge pins.

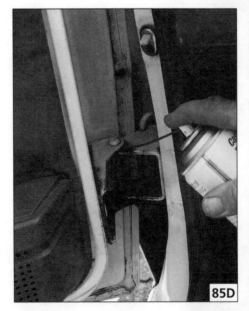

☐ **Job 86. Check aerial.**

86. Work some releasing fluid
into the segments of the aerial,
wiping off dirt. Don't lubricate
with oil since it encourages more
dirt to stick.

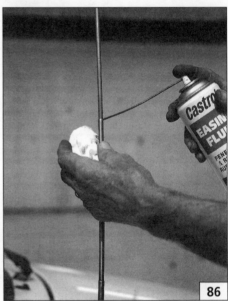

☐ **Job 87. Check seat mountings.**
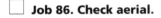

87. Check the seats for security by trying to rock them and check the
seat adjustment mechanism. Grease the runners lightly and wipe off
any surplus to avoid soiling clothes. Check that the folding seat backs
lock securely in the upright position and that the release catches work
smoothly.

You can learn a lot about the condition of an engine from looking at the spark plugs. The following information and photographs, reproduced here with grateful thanks to NGK, show you what to look out for.

1. Good Condition

If the firing end of a spark plug is brown or light grey, the condition can be judged to be good and the spark plug is functioning at its best.

4. Overheating

When having been overheated, the insulator tip can become glazed or glossy, and deposits which have accumulated on the insulator tip may have melted. Sometimes these deposits have blistered on the insulator's tip.

6. Abnormal Wear

Abnormal electrode erosion is caused by the effects of corrosion, oxidation, reaction with lead, all resulting in abnormal gap growth.

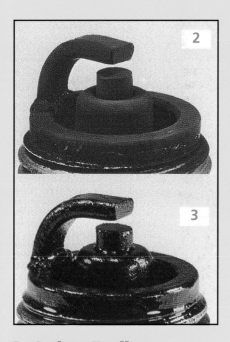

5. Normal Wear

A worn spark plug not only wastes fuel but also strains the whole ignition system because the expanded gap requires higher voltage. As a result, a worn spark plug will result in damage to the engine itself, and will also increase air pollution. The normal rate of gap growth is usually around 'half-a-thou.' or 0.0006 in. every 5,000 miles (0.01 mm. every 5,000 km.).

7. Breakage

Insulator damage is self-evident and can be caused by rapid heating or cooling of the plug whilst out of the car or by clumsy use of gap setting tools. Burned away electrodes are indicative of an ignition system that is grossly out of adjustment. Do not use the car until this has been put right.

2. Carbon Fouling

Black, dry, sooty deposits, which will eventually cause misfiring and can be caused by an over-rich fuel mixture. Check all carburettor settings, choke operation and air filter cleanliness. Clean plugs vigorously with a brass bristled wire brush.

3. Oil Fouling

Oily, wet-looking deposits. This is particularly prone to causing poor starting and even misfiring. Caused by a severely worn engine but do not confuse with wet plugs removed from the engine when it won't start. If the "wetness" evaporates away, it's not oil fouling.

☐ **Job 88. Check seat belts.**

88A. Examine the seat belts for chafing and tug hard at them to check their fixings to the body. With inertia seat belts, check the inertia lock. On some types this can be done just by giving the belt a sharp tug, but others operate only when

the car is under hard deceleration. Test this type on the road but make sure there are no pedestrians nor any other traffic about.

88B. Fit each seat belt catch into its socket and check that it holds properly and frees easily when the catch is pressed. NEVER try to repair a seat belt or its catch, and do not mix catches and sockets from different belts. If you find anything faulty, replace the whole belt and socket.

Every 6,000 miles - Under the Car

☐ **Job 89. Front fuel and brake pipes.**

89. Check all the fuel and brake lines beneath the front end of the car, taking note that corrosion starts at areas exposed to blasting by road dirt, and around and underneath clips. Bend each flexible hose back on itself quite sharply and look for cracks in the surface of the rubber. If you find signs of cracking, or severe corrosion on metal pipes, they need replacing, so seek SPECIALIST SERVICE.

☐ **Job 90. Exhaust system and mountings.**

Check the exhaust manifold and downpipe connections for security and leaks. Also, check the rear of the exhaust system and the rubber suspension straps for security, and the pipe for leaks.

INSIDE INFORMATION: An easy way to locate any leaks in the exhaust system is to get a helper to hold a piece of board over the end of the tailpipe while the engine is ticking over. Any leaks will show up as a hissing sound. Never carry out this check in the garage, always out of doors. Beware! Do not touch the exhaust pipe - there's a risk of being burned!

☐ **Job 91. Front shock absorbers/dampers.**

91. Check the front shock absorbers for any signs of leaks or corrosion. If you find leaks or rusting-through, the shock absorber needs replacing, but always replace them in pairs, never singly, even if only one is faulty.

☐ **Job 92. Steering rack mountings.**

92. Check the security and tightness of the steering rack mountings, a bracket on one side and a U-bolt on the other and also check the connection between the bottom of the steering column and the rack, for tightness.

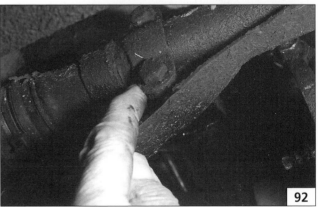

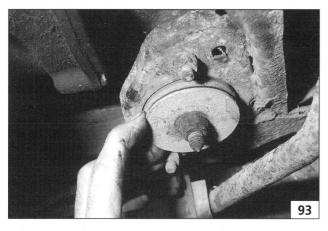

☐ Job 93. Check subframe mountings and engine mountings.

93. Check the subframe mountings and the engine mountings for deterioration of the rubber. These mountings often get soaked in oil (especially at the front) which attacks the rubber. If any of them feels soft and soggy, the mounting needs replacing. NOTE: Pre-1985 Metros have two engine mountings, while 1985 model year-on vehicles have three.

☐ Job 94. Rear brake pipes, fuel pipes and Hydragas suspension pipes.

94. IMPORTANT: Take note of **FACT FILE: HYDRAGAS SUSPENSION,** before Job 37. Check all the pipes under the rear of the car, brake pipes, fuel pipes and pipes joining the Hydragas suspension units. Look for signs of corrosion or deterioration, paying particular attention under clips where corrosion often starts. If you find any, seek **SPECIALIST SERVICE.**

☐ Job 95. Rear shock absorbers.

Check the rear shock absorbers for security and leaks. Always replace them in pairs even if only one is faulty.

☐ Job 96. Rustproofing under the body.

96. Check the bodysealing under the car and, if you find any flaking, scrape it off. If bare metal is exposed, treat it with rust killer and then paint. Renew wax treatment to wheel arches and underbody areas. Refer to *Chapter 5, Rustproofing*, for details.

☐ Job 97. Clear drain holes.

97. Check and clear the drain holes in the doors, sills and sun roof (see inset drawings) if fitted. If you fail to do so, water will gather and body corrosion will take place in very short order! (Illustration, courtesy Rover Group Ltd.)

Every 12,000 Miles - or Every Twelve Months, Whichever Comes First

Every 12,000 miles - The Engine Bay

☐ **Job 98. Breather hoses.**

Check the breather hoses between the engine and air intake for condition and security. If they are blocked it is almost certain that the breather connection on the engine is also blocked. Renew the hoses and clear the obstruction.

1 LITRE HLE ENGINES ONLY

98. Renew the carburettor float chamber vent filter. If this becomes blocked it can lead to uneven running and increased fuel consumption. (Illustration, courtesy Rover Group Ltd)

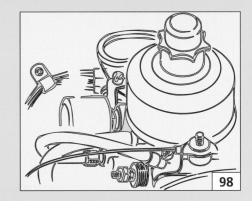

98

☐ **Job 99. Oil filler cap.**

99. Renew the oil filler cap which is part of the breather system and has a non-serviceable breather valve inside.

INSIDE INFORMATION: If you don't, the engine can turn into an oil-burner, even though nothing major is worn. Well worth checking, along with Job 98, if your engine starts to smoke from the exhaust pipe.

☐ **Job 100. Oil leaks.**

Check over the engine carefully for oil leaks, paying particular attention to the area round the crankshaft seals at the front and back of the sump, the mechanical fuel pump, if fitted, the front timing cover and the rocker cover. Generally speaking, leaks will mean dismantling and new gaskets. You will be fitting a new gasket to the rocker cover as part of Job 102 but, if you find leaks at other places and do not feel competent to carry out the dismantling necessary to renew the gasket, seek **SPECIALIST SERVICE**.

99

☐ **Job 101. Clean radiator**

Remove the front grille, and clean any muck and dead flies from the radiator matrix. Use a hose and a soft brush.

☐ **Job 102. Check valve clearances.**

102A. Remove the rocker cover so that you can check the valve clearances.

102B. Adjusting the valve clearances is carried out with the engine cold and they must be set with the tappet on the heel of the cam to give the greatest clearance. The easiest way to set the engine for this is to remember the 'Rule of Nine'.

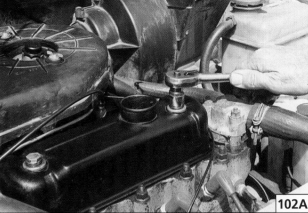

102A

INSIDE INFORMATION: If, after setting the clearances accurately, the tappets are still noisy it probably means that the pads at the ends of the rocker arms are indented, giving a false reading. You can buy a tool at most accessory shops with which you can set the clearances to allow for this indentation.

Alternatively, you can do it with two feeler gauges. First, put any feeler gauge in the gap and screw the adjuster down till the feeler is tight. Then back the adjusting screw off, counting the turns and part turns carefully, till a feeler of the correct thickness will just slide in on top of the first feeler. You now know the number of turns back-off to give the correct clearance, so remove both feelers, screw the adjusting screw down till there is no clearance and back it off by the same number of turns and part turns.. You will now have the correct clearance.

102B

102C

making it easy! When reading the following, remember that number 1 valve is at the 'front' of the engine - the right-hand end when looking at the engine bay from the front of the car.

Remove the sparking plugs to make turning the engine easier, then turn the engine with a spanner on the front of the crankshaft till number 8 valve is fully open. Then set the clearance on valve number 1 (8 plus 1 equals 9). Next, turn the engine till number 7 valve is fully open and set the clearance on valve number 2 (7 plus 2 equals 9). Carry on till all the valve clearances have been set. Set the clearances by slackening the locknut at the end of the rocker arm and turning the adjuster screw till a feeler gauge of the correct thickness (see **Chapter 8, Facts and Figures**) is a firm sliding fit between the top of the valve and the rocker arm.

102C. Clean the inside of the rocker cover and remove all traces of the old gasket. Fit a new gasket.

INSIDE INFORMATION: Fasten the gasket to the rocker cover with gasket jointing compound but don't get any on the face of the gasket. Just smear the face of the gasket with grease. Then, if you have to remove the rocker cover later, the gasket will stay with the cover instead of getting torn or squeezed out of shape.

102D

102D. Also, check the grommets fitted to the rocker cover studs. Don't make the common mistake of over-tightening the cover - it causes leaks - just 'nip' the nuts down onto the top of the cover. Drive the car for several miles until it reaches its normal operating temperature. Check the rocker cover again for leaks.

103A

☐ **Job 103. Clutch stop clearances and mechanism.**

103A. On some models there is a clutch return stop on the clutch release lever with an adjusting screw and locknut. Disconnect the clutch lever return spring and push the lever away from the engine to take up all the free play. Insert a 0.50mm (0.020 in.) feeler gauge between the clutch lever and the screw head. If adjustment is needed, slacken the locknut and turn the screw until the correct clearance is achieved. Re-tighten the locknut and refit the clutch lever return spring.

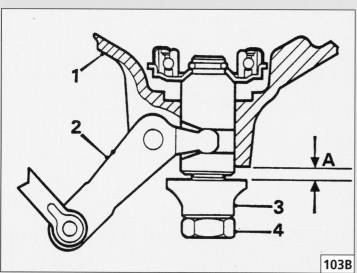

103B

103B. On other models, there is no stop on the clutch release lever but, the clearance is adjusted by turning the large nut on the end of the clutch in the centre of the bell housing (see illustration 103B). Pull the release lever away from the clutch cover until you feel the bearing make light contact. Measure the gap A in 103B. This should be 6.5mm (0.26 in.). If it is not, slacken the locknut (4) and turn the plunger stop (3) until the correct clearance is obtained. Re-tighten the locknut.

MODELS WITH CABLE OPERATED CLUTCHES ONLY

103C. Lubricate the clutch mechanism. Cases of clutch judder on some Metros fitted with self-adjusting cable operated clutched (1985 models-on) have been traced to lack of lubrication of the cable and the throw-out mechanism. The pin joints where the cable attaches to the end of the release lever and the inner cable should be greased, as should the pin where the clutch release lever pivots. It is difficult to grease this pivot pin with ordinary grease without dismantling - consult your workshop manual. If you do not feel competent to undertake any dismantling,

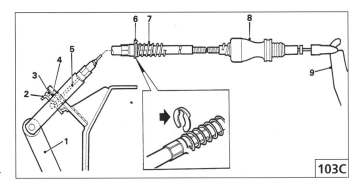

we recommend that you squirt the pivot liberally with an aerosol type spray grease. If this treatment does not cure judder, the fault may lie deeper in the clutch mechanism and it is time to seek **SPECIALIST SERVICE**. (Illustration, courtesy Rover Group Ltd)

☐ Job 104. Cylinder compressions.

> *SAFETY FIRST!*
> *Take off the low tension leads at the coil (the small wires, one each side of the main HT lead to the distributor) so there is no danger of the engine firing nor of electric shock. Carry out this work outside, and make sure that the gearbox is in neutral or 'Park' in the case of automatics.*

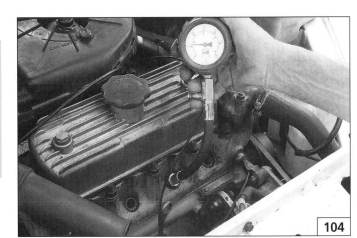

Ensure that the engine oil is up to the recommended level and that the engine is at operating temperature. Remove all the sparking plugs.

104. Screw the compression tester into each plug hole in turn. Open the throttle fully and crank the engine over on the starter motor. Make a note of the maximum reading on the pressure gauge. Check each cylinder in turn and compare the results. If the engine is in good condition there should not be a variation in the readings of more than 5 or 6 psi, 10 at the most.

INSIDE INFORMATION. If you get a low reading on two adjacent cylinders it is an indication that the cylinder head gasket is leaking between the two. If you get low, varied readings, put a teaspoonful of oil in each plug hole and test again. If the readings come up and show much less variation, it means that the pistons rings are worn or sticking and the oil has made a temporary seal. If there is little or no difference in the readings compared with the first test, it means that the valves in the cylinder head are worn and need re-seating or replacing.

Every 12,000 miles - Around the Car

☐ Job 105. Test shock absorbers.

With the car on level ground, 'bounce' each corner in turn and note how the car recovers from the bounce. It should return evenly and smoothly from being pushed down. If it continues to bounce, it means that the shock absorbers are weak and worn out. Always renew them in pairs.

☐ Job 106. Toolkit and jack.

Check that you have at least the minimum toolkit - wheel chocks, wheel brace or hide hammer, jack and warning triangle - for changing a wheel at the roadside if necessary. NOTE: On older cars we do not recommend using the side sill body jack because of the danger of straining the jack mountings in the sills. Our advice is buy - and carry! - an independent hydraulic or scissors jack.

Every 12,000 miles - Under the Car

☐ Job 107. Front suspension bushes.

Check with a pry bar or tyre lever for wear in the front suspension bushes. If you find too much movement, or the ends of the rubber bushes have gone soggy and soft, seek **SPECIALIST SERVICE** as renewing them means depressurising the Hydragas system. Do not attempt to depressurise this at home.

> *SAFETY FIRST!*
> *Raise the car off the ground after reading carefully the information at the start of this chapter on lifting and supporting the car.*

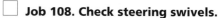

Job 108. Check steering swivels.

108. With the wheel just clear of the ground, and before you put axle stands under the car, use a long lever to try to lift the wheel bodily up and down. If you find any vertical free play, or if the wheel rocks from top to bottom, either the hub bearings are worn or the steering swivel ball joints are probably worn. Seek SPECIALIST SERVICE as renewing the swivels means depressurising the Hydragas system. Do not attempt to depressurise it at home. See FACT FILE: HYDRAGAS SUSPENSION before Job 37.

Job 109. Check steering ball joints and rack.

109. With the wheel still just clear of the ground, grasp it at the sides and try to turn the steering backwards and forwards. If you feel any free play either the ball joints on the ends of the steering rack, or the steering rack itself, are worn. Wait till the car is safely up on axle stands before investigating further.

Job 110. Check steering wheel free play.

110. Check for excessive free play at the steering wheel. If it is present, find out why - check steering ball joints for wear, steering rack for wear and mountings for tightness - or seek SPECIALIST SERVICE. See *Chapter 7, Getting Through the MoT*, for what is and what isn't acceptable.

Job 111. Front calipers.

Examine the front brake calipers to check for leaks. Any sign of leeks means that the caliper must be overhauled or renewed - a SPECIALIST SERVICE job.

Job 112. Rear brake inspection and overhaul.

We recommend that, after fitting new brake shoes, you should avoid heavy braking - except in an emergency - for the first 150-200 miles (250-300 km).

112A. Unscrew the adjuster, anti-clockwise, as far as it will go before trying to remove the drum. Use a proper brake adjusting tool for this, rather than a spanner, as it is less likely to round off the squared end on the adjuster.

112B. Remove the drum by taking out the two cross-head screws.

112C. If the drum does not want to move, tap round its rim with a hide mallet.

112B

INSIDE INFORMATION: On later Metros there is a paper gasket under the drum to stop water entering. This can be fitted to early models - buy them from your Rover dealer.

112D. Check the lining thickness. The maker's recommendation is that new shoes are fitted when the linings are worn down to 1.6mm (0.062 in.) or less. Remember that it will be another 12,000 miles before you inspect them again, so we would recommend 3.2mm (1/8 in.) as an absolute minimum. As you can see, there is plenty of life left in these linings.

Lift back the rubber boot on the hydraulic wheel cylinder and check for any leakage of brake fluid. If you find any, the cylinder needs overhauling or replacing. Unless you are competent in this work, seek **SPECIALIST SERVICE.**

112E. Inspect the inside of the drum for ridging and scoring. Slight scoring is acceptable but, if it is bad, the drum will need renewing. If you are in doubt, seek **SPECIALIST SERVICE.**

112C

☐ Job 113. Renew rear brake shoes.

The hub flange at the rear of a Metro is quite large which makes replacing the brake shoes rather awkward. Attempt it only if you are competent to do so. Whether you renew the shoes or not, squirt all the mechanism and the back plate liberally with a proprietary brake cleaner to remove the dust.

112D

112E

113A. In this line drawing 1 is the adjuster, 2 indicates the brake shoes, 3 the wheel cylinder, 4 the handbrake levers, 5 the lower pull-off spring and 6 the upper pull-off spring. Before removing the shoes, note the location of the two return springs and the holes into which they are hooked. Note that the lower pull-off spring has an offset link between the coils. The spring must be fitted with this link at the bottom so that it does not foul the hub. Note also that the linings are offset on the shoes. The leading edge of each lining - the edge which meets the drum first as the wheel turns in its normal direction of rotation - is set back from the tip of the shoe. (Illustration, courtesy Rover Group Ltd.)

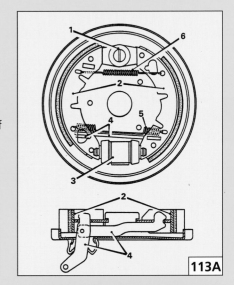

113A

> **SAFETY FIRST!**
> *Before you take the old shoes off, make a note, each side, of how the shoes and springs are positioned. If you get them wrong, the brakes will not work properly, if at all.*

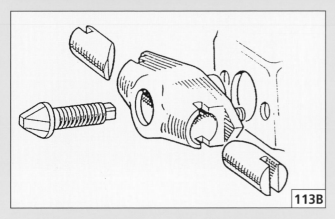

113B

Release each shoe from the adjuster by levering them apart with a stout screwdriver, and then lever the shoes away from the wheel cylinder. Disengage the shoes from the handbrake levers and lift them away complete with their pull-off springs. Put an elastic band or a twisted piece of soft wire round the wheel cylinder to avoid any danger of the pistons falling out. DO NOT apply the footbrake or handbrake while the shoes are off. Clean the backplate with a proprietary brake cleaner.

113B. Note that the adjuster wedges pull out and the adjuster cone screws out forwards. Strip out and re-grease with a small smear of brake grease. If the adjuster needs replacement, it unbolts from the backplate, as shown. (Illustration, courtesy A P Lockheed Ltd.)

Lay the new shoes down on a flat surface and hook the lower pull-off spring in position. Lightly grease the backplates where the shoes rub with special brake grease (NOT ordinary grease!) then fit the shoes and spring to the handbrake levers. Remove the elastic band or wire and locate the shoe webs in the slots in the wheel cylinder. Be careful not to get grease on the linings. Hook the upper pull-off spring in position, remembering that it fits from the back of the shoes, and lever the top webs of the shoes into the slots on the adjuster pegs.

> *making it easy!* However careful you are, there is always a danger of contaminating the new linings with oil or grease from dirty fingers. Cover the linings with masking tape before you start and you won't have to worry about it! Remove the tape once the new shoes are in place.

Tap the shoes till they are centralised, then refit the drum with a new paper gasket and replace the two screws. Once the drums are on, you can centralise the shoes properly by treading hard on the brake pedal several times before adjusting the brakes as given in Job 53.

After adjusting the brakes, refit the wheels and lower the car to the ground.

☐ Job 114. Top-up rustproofing.

Renew and top-up the wax coating to the sills, box sections, insides of doors and underside of car. See *Chapter 5, Rustproofing,* for full details.

Every 24,000 Miles - or Every Twenty Four Months, Whichever Comes First

The Service Jobs listed below should be carried out in addition to the regular 12,000 mile/twelve month Service Jobs shown previously. They cover the areas which experience has shown can give trouble in the longer term or, in some cases, they cover areas that may prevent trouble starting in the first place. Many of them don't appear on manufacturer's service schedules, but they are the sort of jobs that can make the difference between a car that is reliable and one that gives trouble out of the blue.

Every 24,000 miles - The Engine Bay

SAFETY FIRST!
*Read carefully the information in **Chapter 1, Safety First!** especially that regarding the safety hazards surrounding petrol (gasoline). Mop up any fuel which is spilt when you change the filter, have a workshop-sized fire extinguisher handy and make sure it is the type which can be used on petrol fires. Because of the fire risk, carry out this operation out of doors. Disconnect the battery before disconnecting the filter - see FACT FILE on page 23.*

☐ Job 115. Change fuel filter.

MG METRO TURBO MODELS ONLY

MG Metro Turbo models have a fuel filter in the fuel line between the pressure regulator and the carburettor. Release the hose clips either side of the filter and ease the hoses off. Inspect the hoses and clips and, if necessary, renew them. When you fit the new filter, look for either an arrow indicating the direction of flow, or the words OUT and IN. If the filter is marked with an arrow, this should point towards the carburettor. If the words OUT and IN are marked, OUT should be towards the carburettor, and IN should be towards the pressure regulator.

☐ Job 116. Drain and refill cooling system.

SAFETY FIRST!
Work on the cooling system only when the engine is cold. If you drain a system when the engine is hot, the remaining coolant inside can boil over and release scalding water and steam.

116. Remove the pressure cap, open the heater valve and drain the system by undoing the bottom radiator hose. On some models there is also a drain plug at the back of the block, approximately in the middle.

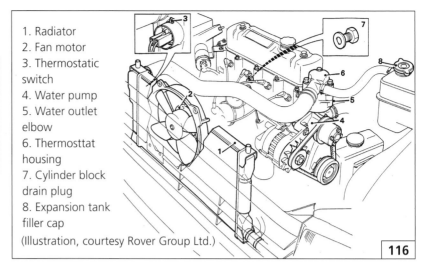

1. Radiator
2. Fan motor
3. Thermostatic switch
4. Water pump
5. Water outlet elbow
6. Thermosttat housing
7. Cylinder block drain plug
8. Expansion tank filler cap
(Illustration, courtesy Rover Group Ltd.)

116

After draining the system, flush it through with cold water. With the cap still off and the plug still out, put a garden hose into the bottom radiator hose and plug around it with rags. Turn on the water and let it run until no more sediment or discoloured water comes out. Open and close the heater tap from time to time to help the water surge through and flush the heater. If you suspect the heater is heavily sedimented, disconnect the hoses and flush it through separately.

Refill the system, first checking in *Chapter 8, Facts and Figures,* to establish the capacity of the cooling system. Mix sufficient water and antifreeze in a 50/50 solution. Replace the drain plug, if fitted, and fill through the expansion tank to the level indicated on the side of the tank.

Replace the filler plug and pressure cap, start the engine and let it run to circulate the coolant. Wait for the engine to cool right down, then check the coolant level again. Check it yet again when it has cooled down after a run on the road.

INSIDE INFORMATION: Remember that antifreeze, even in diluted form, will attack paintwork. Be particularly careful when flushing and if you have to disconnect the heater hoses. Any spilt antifreeze should be washed off immediately with plenty of cold water.

☐ Job 117. Renew radiator pressure cap.

Renew the radiator pressure cap at this stage even it looks in good condition. The spring weakens in time and releases coolant earlier than it should so your engine could overheat. Check the poundage of the new cap to make sure it is the same as the old one. It should be stamped on the top.

☐ Job 118. Renew alternator/fan belt.

Renew fan belt - refer to Job 32. It's not worth running the risk of a breakdown. Regard renewal at this stage as an investment.

☐ Job 119. Change brake servo filter.

119. Many models are equipped with an in-line brake vacuum servo unit fitted between the brake pedal and the master cylinder. Ease back the rubber book (119.1) covering the servo push-rod and hook out the old filter (119.2) from the end of the servo unit. Cut the new filter so it can be fitted over the push-rod and ease it back into the servo body. Refit the rubber boot. (Illustration, courtesy Rover Group Ltd.)

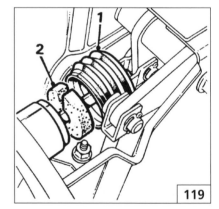

119

☐ Job 120. Check air intake flap.

On most models, there is a simple flap operated by a bi-metallic strip, inside the air filter housing. With the filters removed (see Job 33), the bi-metallic strip will be seen. Play a hot-air hair dryer on it; the head should cause the flap to direct air through the hot-air inlet (via the exhaust manifold). If it doesn't work, you'll have to replace the whole housing.

MG1300, GTA AND SPORT MODELS ONLY

120. On other models, there's a more complex arrangement. A small temperature operated valve (1) opens the 'suction' pipes connected to the inlet manifold and the diverter flap (2). Check that all connections are sound. Disconnect the trunking (3) and check visually that the flap supplies heated air when the engine is cold but colder air when the engine is hot, in warm weather. (Illustration, courtesy Rover Group Ltd.)

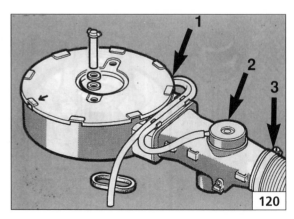

120

Every 24,000 miles - Under the Car

☐ Job 121. Flushing oil.

On older engines where you don't know the service history it could be a good idea to drain and flush the oil at this service. Generally, though, flushing will not be necessary on engines which have had regular oil changes. Drain the old oil, but leave the oil filter in place. Fill the engine with proprietary flushing oil and follow the instructions on the can. Generally these will say run the engine for five minutes or so after it reaches its normal operating temperature. Don't rev the engine unduly, and never drive it on the road, with flushing oil in the sump. Drain the flushing oil out, change the filter and refill with new oil as detailed in Job 41.

☐ Job 122. Suspension mountings.

Check the tightness of all the bolts of the front suspension.

123

☐ Job 123. Brake discs.

SAFETY FIRST! and SPECIALIST SERVICE
*Obviously, a car's brakes are among its most important safety related items. Do not dismantle your car's brakes unless you are fully competent to do so. If you have not been trained in this work, but wish to carry out the work described here, we strongly recommend that you have a garage or qualified mechanic check your work before using the car on the road. See also the section on BRAKES AND ASBESTOS in **Chapter 1**, for further important information.*

To measure the brake disc thickness, undo the brake caliper retaining bolts, slide the caliper, complete with pads off the disc, and tie it up under the wheel arch using string or wire. Take care not to stretch the brake hydraulic hose.

123. Use a micrometer to measure the thickness of the brake discs. If you don't own one, this is **SPECIALIST SERVICE**. If the thickness varies considerably around various points on the discs, replace with new discs. If the discs are badly scored, you may be able to have an engineering shop skim them down for you. (Ask them to check that the discs run true before spending on them.) But you will probably find it less expensive, to buy replacement discs.

☐ Job 124. Renew brake fluid.

Over a period of time, brake fluid absorbs moisture from the air and, should the fluid at the calipers or wheel cylinders get very hot with prolonged braking, this water can boil and cause a vapour lock - in other words, completely inoperative brakes! **If this job is not carried out properly it can result in brakes which could let you down without warning.**

Do not carry out this job unless you have been trained to do it, and do not attempt it without the workshop manual as procedures differ on different models of car. We strongly recommend that you regard this as a **SPECIALIST SERVICE** and leave the job to your Rover dealer. They have equipment which can do the job quickly and thoroughly.

Every 24,000 miles - Around the Car

☐ Job 125. Window regulators.

Remove the trim from the inside of the doors and check and lubricate the window regulating mechanism. Apply silicone grease to the window channelling inside the door.

☐ **Job 126. Door gear.**

While the trim is off, lubricate the inside of the door locks and pull mechanism.

☐ **Job 127. Light seals.**

127. Remove all the light lenses and check the condition of the rubber seals. Renew any that are split or perished.

127

Every 36,000 Miles - or Every thirty Six Months, Whichever Comes First

Carry out all the Jobs listed under earlier service headings before carrying out these tasks.

☐ **Job 128. Renew distributor cap and leads.**

Renew the distributor cap and high tension leads. Using the old cap and the recess for the locating tag as a guide, mark the turrets of the new cap 1, 2, 3 and 4, either with numbers on slips of masking tape or with typewriter correcting fluid, so you do not fit the new leads in the wrong order.

INSIDE INFORMATION: If you make a mistake, or loose the order, you can set it again. Put the rotor arm on, but leave the cap off, and turn the engine, noting which way the rotor arm is turning, until number 1 cylinder is on its firing stroke. You can check this by removing the plug, putting your thumb over the plug hole and feeling for the pressure of compression.

Alternatively, remove the rocker cover and check that both valves of number 1 cylinder have clearance. Turn the engine to top dead centre by checking the timing marks, offer up the new cap and check the stud to which the rotor arm is pointing. This will be the stud for number 1 lead. The firing order is 1, 3, 4, 2 so, going round the cap the same way as the rotor arm turns, the remaining four turrets will take the leads for number 3, number 4 and number 2 plugs respectively.

☐ **Job 129. Float chamber.**

NON-TURBO CARS ONLY

129. Remove the float chamber from the carburettor and clean out any sediment - refer to Job 75.

> **SAFETY FIRST!**
> **Do not carry out this check on Turbo carburettors without seeking SPECIALIST SERVICE. They are pressurised up to 7 lb/sq.in. and removing the cover could cause a nasty accident!**

☐ **Job 130. Rear hubs.**

> **SAFETY FIRST!**
> **Raise the rear of the car only after reading carefully the information at the start of this Chapter on lifting and supporting the car.**

129

Lever the grease retainer caps from the middle of the rear hubs, and clean them out. Fill them one quarter full with new high melting point grease and tap them back on.

CHAPTER 4 - BODYWORK

In this Chapter, we show you how to make your car look its best. First, we demonstrate that your car's appearance can be improved beyond recognition by a couple of hours of work on a Sunday morning. Then, just in case a passing gate post should leap out at you, we explain how to carry out simple bodywork repairs at home.

PART I: THE BODY BEAUTIFUL

Have you ever looked in amazement at the condition of cars on a dealer's forecourt and wondered why your car doesn't look like that? Well, it can! It's all a matter of know-how and a bit of hard work - and using the techniques described in this Chapter, you'll find that your car can be made to look almost like new again, without using too many cans of elbow grease!

☐ I.2 Weekend trips in your car are likely to be cursed by the 'bugs on the bumper' syndrome, as well as black tar on the bodywork. Soak all the bug-splatted areas with soapy water first, while you wash the rest of the car, then come back later, when they've been softened. Rub off with cloth, rather than a sponge. Use a proprietary brand of tar remover to wipe off tar splash.

☐ I.1 Apply a thin coat of modern car polish, to give a far longer-lasting shine than old-fashioned waxes (though we've yet to find one that lasts as long as claimed!). Cover just one section of the car at a time and then, as soon as the wax dries to a haze, buff off for a superb shine. You'll see the dull paint and oxides come off on the cloth as you buff.

I.1

SOFT-TOP SPORTS CARS: If your vinyl soft-top has ingrained dirt, scrub it gently all over with a nail brush and soapy water. When dry, apply a good quality vinyl cleaner to bring the appearance back like new. Fabric soft-tops should only be washed, not scrubbed, but can be hosed off to shift the dirt.

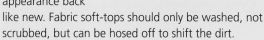

I.2

making it easy!
• As you polish, keep turning the cloth, always presenting a clean face to the surface of the paint - that's the secret of obtaining a clear shine with no rub marks. You'll need several clean cloths for polishing a whole car!

• Try removing a bug splat with a kitchen abrasive pad - the gentler sort made for non-stick pans - but only on glass and chrome; it'll ruin the shine on paintwork.

☐ I.3 It's easy to forget that around a fifth of your car's 'bodywork' is in fact glass. Use purpose-made glass cleaner, or a clean wash leather, for sparkling results. Clouding on the inside (said to be the vapour from upholstery plastics!) cleans off in the same way.

I.3

BODYWORK

☐ I.4 Tyres are one of the most 'visual' parts of your car. There are proprietary tyre polishes and paints available, but be warned that the improvement in appearance goes the first time you drive on a wet road! A good cleaning with the wash sponge - *after* you've washed the rest of the car - is usually enough. Alloy wheels need a spray-on alloy wheel cleaner to shift stuck-on brake dust.

☐ I.5 INSIDE INFORMATION: Many people just don't know what to do about dull plastic bumpers. Use a colourless trim cleaner and you'll find that just wiping it on will bring about a magical improvement. Several coats may be needed. (The old, black-coloured bumper polish makes a real mess of your hands, by the way!)

I.4

☐ I.6 Even when an engine bay is clean, it often looks dirty. Use a spray-on cleaner to remove the heavy dirt and grease - best if you let it soak in to the worst areas. Use an old paintbrush in nooks and crannies. A vinyl protectant will then bring up a wonderful sheen to all of your hoses and pipes as well as all underbonnet paintwork.

making it easy! If your engine is very oily, ask a local garage with a steam cleaner to hose off the worst of the 'grunge' before starting to clean up the engine bay. Paint any bare metal exposed by the steam cleaning, before it starts to rust.

☐ I.7 Choose a vinyl cleaner designed to put back the suppleness into vinyl and protect it from fading, as well as to remove dirt and grime and restore the appearance. If you hate the 'tacky' high gloss shine produced by some of them, look out for the low-gloss variety, giving a more natural finish.

I.5

INSIDE INFORMATION: If you can't get hold of low-gloss vinyl cleaner, try wiping over with a damp cloth before the cleaner has fully dried. This also 'wipes' away the worst of the gloss.

Rubber seals will last far longer if they are protected against the elements, by regular treatments with vinyl and rubber protectant. Scrape out dirt and grit from around the lower door seals then treat them all with several coats.

☐ I.8 Fabric seats and carpets will certainly benefit from cleaning with a proprietary brand of spray-on car upholstery cleaner - or a household upholstery cleaner. Follow the instructions carefully, take care not to soak cloth trim (it could cause shrinking) and the result will be carpets and cloth seats that look like new.

I.6

You can make leather more supple, and keep it cleaner and longer lasting by using a purpose-made brand of leather care. After use, the leather will feel soft and supple, because of the lanolin and moisturisers that you will have added. At first, you may be surprised to see the colour of your leather go much darker but don't worry; that will pass as the leather cleaner dries out naturally.

I.7

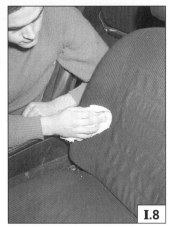
I.8

PART II: REPAIRING BODYWORK BLEMISHES

However well you look after your car, there will always be the risk of car park accident damage - or even worse! The smallest paint chips are best touched up with paint purchased from your local auto. accessory shop. If your colour of paint is not available, some auto. accessory shops offer a mixing scheme (including aerosols, in some cases) or you could look for a local paint factor in Yellow Pages. Take your car along to the paint factor and have them match the colour and mix the smallest quantity of cellulose paint that they will supply you with. Larger body blemishes will need the use of body filler.

II.1

SAFETY FIRST!
***Always** wear plastic gloves when working with body filler, before it has set. **Always** wear a face mask when sanding filler and wear goggles when using a power sander.*

☐ II.1 The rear of this car's bodywork has sustained a nasty gash, the sort of damage for which you will certainly need to use body filler. The first stage is to mask off. Try to find "natural" edges such as body mouldings or styling stripes and wherever you can, mask off body trim rather than having to remove it.

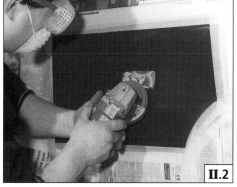

II.2

☐ II.2 Remove all paint from the damaged area and for about 25mm (1 in.) around the damaged area. Roughen the bare metal or surface with coarse abrasive paper - a power sander is best. Wipe over the area with white spirit (mineral spirit) and then wash off with washing-up liquid in water - *not* car wash detergent.

INSIDE INFORMATION: Rub the surrounding paintwork with cutting compound so that the new paint has a better chance of matching the old.

☐ II.3 Mix the filler and hardener, following the instructions on the can. It's best to use a piece of plastic or metal rather than cardboard because otherwise, the filler will pick up fibres from the surface of the card. Mix thoroughly until the colour is consistent and no traces of hardener can be discerned.

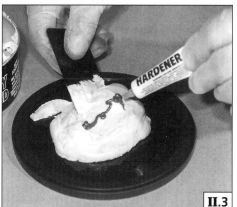

II.3

☐ II.4 You can now spread the filler evenly over the repair. If the damage is particularly deep, apply the paste in two or more layers, allowing the filler to harden before adding the next layer. The final layer should be just proud of the level required, but do not overfill as this wastes paste and will require more time to sand down.

☐ II.5 It is essential when sanding down that you wrap the sanding paper around a flat block. You can see from the scratch marks that this repair has been sanded diagonally in alternate directions until the filler has become level with the surrounding panel, but you have to take care not to go deeply into the edges of the paint around the repair.

INSIDE INFORMATION: There will invariably be small pin holes even if the right

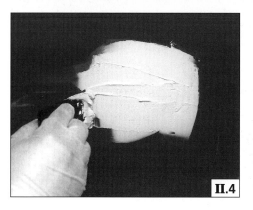

II.4

II.5

amount of filler was applied first time. Use a tiny amount of filler scraped very thin over the whole repair, filling in deep scratches and pin holes and then sanding off with a very fine grade of sand paper - preferably dry paper rather than wet-or-dry because you don't want to get water on to the bare filler.

☐ II.6 You can now use an aerosol primer to spray over the whole area of the repair but preferably not right up to the edges of the masking tape...

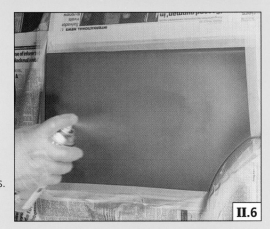

II.6

☐ II.7 ...and now use wet-or-dry paper, again on a sanding block, to sand the primer paint.

INSIDE INFORMATION: Don't sand fresh primer paint - leave it up to a day to harden off.

The filler is now protected from the water by the paint. If you do apply paint right up to the edge of the tape, be sure to 'feather' the edges of the primer, so that the edges blend in smoothly to the surrounding surface, with no ridges.

II.7

SAFETY FIRST!
Always wear an efficient mask when spraying aerosol paint and only work in a well-ventilated area, well away from any source of ignition, because spray paint vapour, even that given off by an aerosol, is highly flammable. Ensure that you have doors and windows open to the outside when using aerosol paint but in cool or damp weather, close them when the vapour has dispersed, otherwise the surface of the paint will "bloom", or take on a milky appearance. In fact, you may find it difficult to obtain a satisfactory finish in cold or damp weather.

☐ II.8 Before starting to spray, ensure that the nozzle is clear. Note that the can must be held with the index finger well back on the aerosol button. If you let your finger overhang the front of the button, a paint drip can form and throw itself on to the work area as a paint blob.

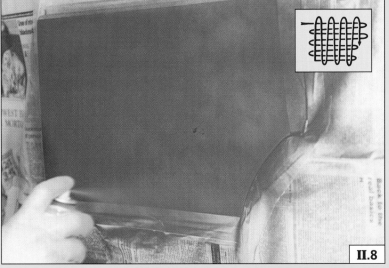

II.8

making it easy! • *One of the secrets of spraying paint which doesn't run, is to put a very light coat of spray paint on to the panel first, followed by several more coats, allowing time between each coat for the bulk of the solvent to evaporate.*

• *Alternate coats should go on horizontally, followed by vertical coats as shown on the inset diagram.*

☐ II.9 After allowing about a week for the paint to dry, you will be able to polish it with a light cutting compound, blending the edges of the repair into the surrounding paintwork.

*INSIDE INFORMATION: Do note that if your repairs don't work out first time and you have to apply more paint on top of the fresh paint that you have already used, allow a week to elapse otherwise there is a strong risk of pickling or other reactions to take place. Also note that a prime cause of paint failure is the existence of silicones on the surface of the old paint before you start work. These come from most types of polish and are not all that easy to remove - they **won't** sand off!. Thoroughly wipe the panel down with white spirit before starting work and wash off with warm water and washing-up liquid to remove any further traces of the polish and the white spirit - but don't use the sponge or bucket that you normally use for washing the car otherwise you will simply introduce more silicones onto the surface!*

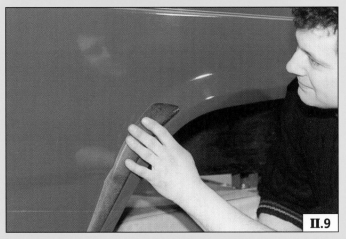

II.9

CHAPTER 5 - RUSTPROOFING

When mechanical components deteriorate, they can cost you a lot of money to replace. But when your car's bodywork deteriorates, it can cost you the car, if corrosion goes beyond the point where repairs are economical to carry out. Rust prevention should be regarded as a regular maintenance job, one which enables you to extend the life of your car by many years - and that will save you *real* money!

If you want to prolong its life, you'll have to inject rustproofing fluid into all the enclosed box sections and 'chassis' sections on your car. In many cases, you'll find holes already in place; in others, you'll be able to take off a cover, a piece or trim or a door lock in order to gain access. But in quite a few cases, you'll need to drill holes to gain an entry.

Choose Your Weapon

Those hand pump injectors that you can buy from DIY shops are often worse than useless. They don't usually make a proper spray, but simply squirt a jet of fluid that does nothing to give the all-over cover required. Make a dummy 'box section' out of a cardboard box - cut it and fold to make it about 10 or 15 cm square - and try a dummy run. Open up and see if it has worked. If you haven't obtained full misting of the fluid, you could be making the problem worse.

INSIDE INFORMATION: Rust strikes even harder in those areas that aren't properly covered!

Consider taking your car to a garage with suitable equipment and having them do the work for you. Full, professional injection equipment, as shown in the following picture sequence, will make the fluid reach much further and deeper than amateur equipment, and if you enlist the services of the best experts as featured here, you'll be able to benefit from their experience.

Don't be a drip!

*INSIDE INFORMATION: i) Place **lots** of newspaper beneath the car to catch the inevitable drips. ii) Some seat belts retract into a cavity that you will want to spray with fluid. Pull each belt out and hold it there until you have finished spraying the fluid. iii) All electric motors should be covered up with plastic bags so that none of the rustproofing fluid gets in and all windows should be fully wound up. iv) Ensure that all drain channels are clear so that any excess rustproofing fluid can drain out and also check once again that they are clear after you have finished carrying out the work to ensure that your application of the fluid has not caused them to be clogged up, otherwise water will become trapped, negating much of the good work you have carried out.*

• A compressor-driven gun of this type won't break the bank - try your local motor trade parts factors - but you'll need to buy or hire a compressor. Results will be perfect.
• Decide on your drill size with reference to the size of the injector nozzle and the size of grommets that you can obtain for blanking the holes off again afterwards. You'll feel a bit foolish if you drill first, only to find that they don't make grommets to fit the holes you've drilled!

SAFETY FIRST!
*Before using rustproofer, read the manufacturer's safety notes. Keep rustproofing fluid off the exhaust or any other components where it could be ignited. Keep it away from brake components, covering them up with plastic bags before starting work. Follow **Chapter 1, Safety First!**, and advice at the start of **Chapter 3, Servicing Your Car** especially with regard to safe working beneath a car raised off the ground. Rustproofers all contain solvents. In a confined space, such as a garage, solvents can build up, creating both a health and a fire hazard. Wear an efficient face mask so that you don't inhale vapour and work out of doors, keeping out of confined spaces. Wear gloves and goggles, but if you do get any fluid in your eyes, wash out with copious amounts of water and immediately seek medical advice if necessary. If any welding has to be carried out on the vehicle within a few months of rustproofing being carried out, you must inform those who are carrying out the work because of the fire risk.*

Our thanks are due to Dinol Ltd for carrying out the work, using Dinitrol rustproofing fluid.

☐ **Job 1. Clean underbody.**

1. You will have to hose off the underside of the body, paying particular attention to the undersides of the wings and wheel arches, before you can start to apply new rust-proofing. Scrape off any hard, thick deposits of mud, and any old flaking body sealant under the car. One of the quickest ways to do the job is to use a power washer with a long lance. Many garages have this equipment for customer use in a wash bay and this is a very efficient way of doing the job. You will, however, still have to go underneath with a scraper afterwards as even a power jet won't take off flaking body sealant. You will also have to wait up to a week for the underside of the car to dry thoroughly (in warm, dry weather) before applying new rustproofing.

1

☐ **Job 2. Equipment.**

2. Gather together all the materials you need to do the job before you start. You will also need lifting equipment and axle stands.

Bear in mind the safety equipment you will need - referred to in ***Safety First!*** - see above. You will need copious amounts of newspaper to spread on the floor because quite a lot of rustproofing fluid will run out of the box sections and other areas under the car and you may have to park your car over newspaper for a couple of days after carrying out this treatment. Remember that the vapour given off by the materials will continue for several days, so park your car in the open for a week or so if you can, rather than in an enclosed garage.

INSIDE INFORMATION: Tip from Dinol, the manufacturers of Dinitrol: Except in a heat wave, it is essential to stand the container of rustproofer in a tub of hot water to keep it fluid. Top up the tub from time to time with more hot water while you are working. Not only will warm rustproofer penetrate seams better, it will flow through the applicator better and not clog so easily. Some people thin the rustproofer with white spirit, but warming it is better. Wash the gun and lances out with white spirit afterwards. If you let the rustproofer set, it is almost impossible to clean them.

Around the Car

☐ **Job 3. Chrome trim and seams.**

Some rustproofing fluids in aerosol cans are thin enough for injecting behind chromium trim strips and badges but some people find that they are inclined to leave a stain on the paintwork around the trim. As an alternative to a rust-proofing fluid, you can use a water dispersant or a thin oil.

4A

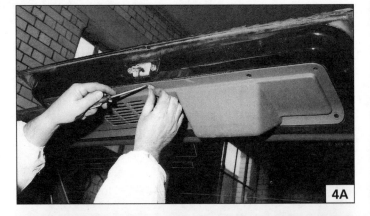

☐ **Job 4. Tailgate.**

4A. Remove the trim panel from behind the tailgate lock, carefully prising out the trim clips with a screwdriver...

4B... and use a flexible pipe to inject rustproofing fluid into all the double skinned areas. At the hinge panel, inject fluid through the horizontal fresh air ventilation slots to cover the vulnerable areas around the hinges.

4B

4C. Below the tailgate, remove the rear lamp clusters and inject fluid into the closed rear skirt behind the bumper.

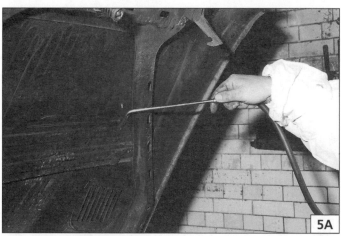

☐ **Job 5. Bonnet.**

5A. There are access areas in all the double skinned and box sections under the bonnet. Inject fluid into all of them...

5B. ...paying particular attention to the nose of the bonnet where condensation and rainwater collects inside.

☐ **Job 6. Inner front wings and bulkhead.**

6A. There are access grommets in the inner front wings, a large one, shown here, being levered out with a screwdriver, and a smaller one behind it.

6B. Run a flexible pipe forward through the larger one and backward and downward through the smaller one to coat all the vulnerable cavities behind the inner wing.

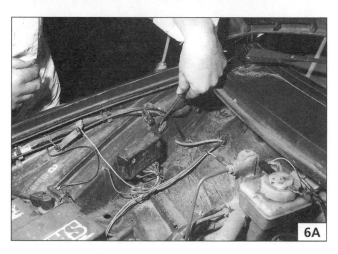

6C. At the back of the inner wing, feed your lance across the car under the bulkhead panel by the wiper spindle and inject fluid across the closed cavity at the base of the windscreen.

6C

6D. Don't forget the underside of the joint, where the front wing is bolted to the front of the bodywork.

6D

☐ Job 7. Sills.

7A. There's no need to drill the sills on a Metro, all the rust-proofing is carried out from inside the car. Remove the front seat belt inertia reels from the their anchorages to avoid coating them with fluid...

7B. ...and then use a long flexible pipe through the aperture, working along back and front, to coat the insides of the sills thoroughly. You can also treat the door shut pillar from the same aperture.

7A

☐ Job 8. Doors and door pillars.

8A. A professional will probably drill holes in the edge of the door to get his lance in because it's quicker than removing the trim, but their position has to be accurately measured, and you can do the job at home more easily and thoroughly by taking the trim panel off.

7B

8A

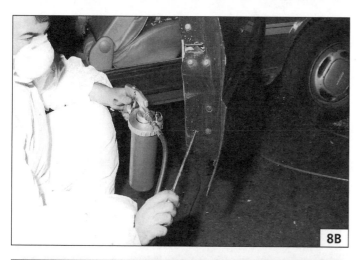

8B

8B. Pay particular attention to the bottom of the door where water collects.

8C. To reach inside the front pillars, take out the courtesy light switch.

8D. There is also an access hole just in front of, and above, the top hinge.

8C

Job 9. Inside rear wheel arches.

9. The double skinning of the rear wheel arches is a rust trap. Inject fluid into the forward part through the aperture where the rear seat belt inertia reels anchor. You can gain access to the rearward part by lifting back the trim inside the luggage compartment.

Under the Car

Job 10. Under-floor box sections.

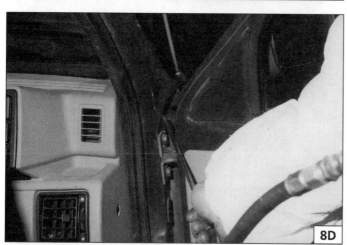

8D

INSIDE INFORMATION: Think carefully before drilling holes to insert rustproofing fluid, especially in the "chassis", where there are numerous holes already. If you do drill a hole in steel, make sure that you file off the rough burrs and then apply an anti-rusting agent, followed by a coating of paint followed by a layer of wax. Make sure the area you drill into is indeed hollow and not the inside of the car or luggage bay! Spend time looking out for wires or pipes. Disconnect the car's battery.

10A. All the box sections under a Metro have drain holes into which you can push your flexible pipe. Push it in as far as you can and inject fluid while you withdraw it.

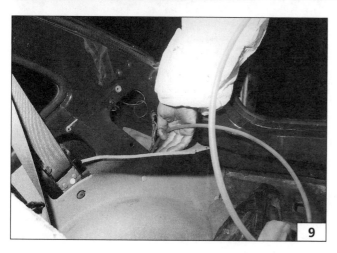

9

10A

10B. There are a number of small box section reinforcing sections...

10C. ...and a whole host of nooks, crannies and seams to be injected.

10D. As well as the chassis sections, inject fluid along the inside of the front skirt through access holes at each side just in front of the anti-roll bar.

☐ **Job 11. Underside of the floor panels.**

11A. Make sure there is no loose or flaking old underseal on the panels. Wear goggles while you scrape any off and while you spray. Spray all the seams and joins under the car with the thinner 'creeping' fluid...

11B. ...and then coat the whole of the underside with the thicker, tough material otherwise the thinner stuff, which is capable of creeping into the seams, will be washed away again. Coat the metal brake and suspension pipes, but try not to coat the exhaust system. It won't do any harm, but it might smell for a time until it burns off.

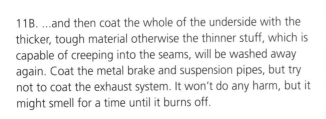

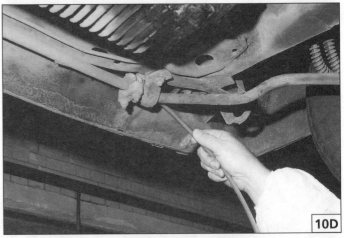

CHAPTER 6 - FAULT FINDING

This Chapter aims to help you to overcome the main faults that can affect the mobility or safety of your vehicle. It also helps you to overcome the problem that has affected most mechanics - amateur and professional - at one time or another... Blind Spot Syndrome!

It goes like this: the vehicle refuses to start one damp Sunday morning. You decide that there must be no fuel getting through. By the time you've stripped the fuel pump and fuel lines and "unblocked" the fuel tank, it's time for bed. And the next day, the local garage finds that your main HT lead has dropped out of the coil! Something like that has happened to most of us!

Don't jump to conclusions: if your engine won't start or runs badly, if electrical components fail, follow the logical sequence of checks listed here and detailed overleaf, eliminating each "check" (by testing, not by "hunch") before moving on to the next. And remember that the great majority of failures are caused by electrical or ignition faults: only a minor proportion of engine failures come from the fuel system. Follow the sequences shown here - and you'll have a better chance of success in finding that fault. Before carrying out any of the work described in this Chapter please read carefully *Chapter 1, Safety First!*

Engine won't start.

1. Starter motor doesn't turn.

2. Is battery okay?

3. Check battery connections for cleanliness/tightness.

4. Have battery 'drop' test carried out by specialist.

5. Test battery with voltmeter or, preferable, with a hydrometer.

6. Can engine be rotated by hand?

7. If engine cannot be rotated by hand, check for mechanical seizure of power unit, or pinion gear jammed in mesh with flywheel - 'rock' car backwards and forwards until free, or apply spanner to square drive at front end of starter motor.

8. If engine can be rotated by hand, check for loose electrical connections at starter, faulty solenoid, or defective starter motor.

9. Starter motor turns slowly.

10. Battery low on charge or defective - re-charge and have 'drop' test carried out by specialist.

11. Internal fault within starter motor - e.g. worn brushes.

12. Starter motor noisy or harsh.

13. Drive teeth on ring gear or starter pinion worn/broken.

14. Main drive spring broken.

15. Starter motor securing bolts loose.

16. Starter motor turns engine but car will not start. See 'Ignition System' box.

Ignition system.

> **SAFETY FIRST!**
> It is essential that you read **Chapter 1, Safety First!, The Ignition System** before carrying out work on this part of the car.

(Carry out the following checks as appropriate. For example, some vehicles have contact breaker ignition while the majority of modern cars have electronic ignition. Only Step 17 can be carried out on cars with electronic ignition. If any faults are found - **SPECIALIST SERVICE**.)

17. Check for spark at plug (remove plug and prop it with threads resting on bare metal of cylinder block). Do not touch plug or lead while operating starter.

MODELS WITHOUT ELECTRONIC IGNITION ONLY

18. If no spark present at plug, check for spark at contact breaker points when 'flicked' open (ignition 'on'). Double-check to ensure that points are clean and correctly gapped, and try again.

19. If spark present at contact breaker points, check for spark at central high tension lead from

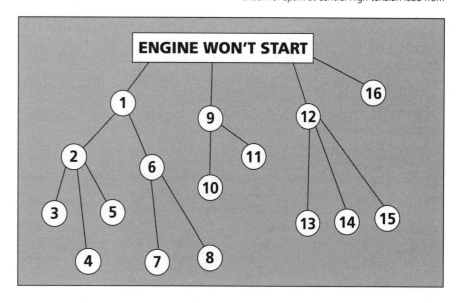

FAULT FINDING

coil. NOTE: Don't carry out this check with electronic ignition systems. An uncontrolled spark can, in some cases, seriously damage the ECU (Electronic Control Unit).

20. If spark present at central high tension lead from coil, check distributor cap and rotor arm; replace if cracked or contacts badly worn.

21. If distributor cap and rotor arm are okay, check high tension leads and connections - replace leads if they are old, carbon core type suppressed variety.

22. If high tension leads are sound but dirty or damp, clean/dry them.

23. If high tension leads okay, check/clean/dry/re-gap sparking plugs.

24. Damp conditions? Apply water dispellant spray to ignition system.

25. If no spark present at contact breaker points (cars without electronic ignition only), examine connections of low tension leads between ignition switch and coil, and from coil to contact breaker (including short low-tension lead within distributor).

26. If low tension circuit connections okay, examine wiring.

27. If low tension wiring is sound, is capacitor okay? If in doubt, fit new capacitor.

28. If capacitor is okay, check for spark at central high tension lead from coil. NOTE: DON'T carry out this check with electronic ignition systems. An uncontrolled spark can, in some cases, seriously damage the ECU (Electronic Control Unit).

29. If no spark present at central high tension lead from coil, check for poor high tension lead connections.

30. If high tension lead connections okay, is coil okay? If in doubt, fit new coil.

31. If spark present at plug, is it powerful or weak? If weak, see '27' (non-electronic ignition models only).

32. If spark is healthy, check ignition timing.

33. If ignition timing is okay, see 'Fuel System' box.

Fuel system.

FUEL INJECTED ENGINES ONLY

34. Do not disconnect fuel pipes to check fuel flow, as system is pressurised; check fuel pump operation by listening for "buzz" when ignition is switched on - buzz should last no more than 1 or 2 seconds; if longer, suspect fuel pump. If no buzz, suspect fuel pump relay - seek professional help.

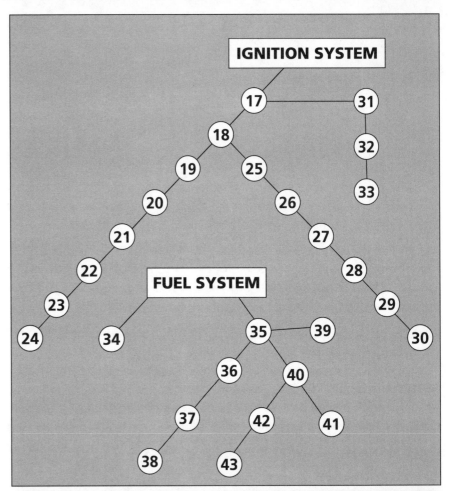

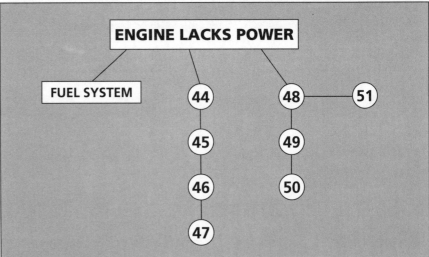

NON FUEL INJECTED ENGINES ONLY

35. Check briefly for fuel at feed pipe to carb. See 36. If no fuel present at feed pipe, is petrol tank empty? (Rock car and listen for 'sloshing' in tank, as well as looking at gauge).

36. Check for a defective fuel pump. With outlet pipe disconnected AND AIMED AWAY FROM HOT EXHAUST COMPONENTS, ETC. as well as your eyes and clothes, and into a suitable container, turn the engine over (manual

*SAFETY FIRST! Before working on the fuel system, read **Chapter 1, Safety First!** Take special care to 1) only work out of doors, 2) wear suitable gloves and goggles and keep fuel out of eyes and away from skin: 3) if fuel does come into contact with skin, wash off straight away, 4) if fuel gets into your eyes, wash out with copious amounts of clean, cold water. Seek medical advice if necessary, 5) when testing for fuel flow, pump into a sufficiently large container, minimising splashes, 6) don't smoke, work near flames or sparks or work when the engine or exhaust are hot.*

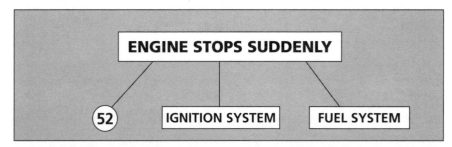

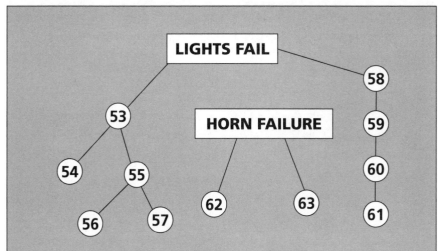

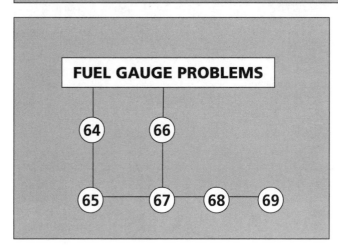

47. If oil level okay, check for slipping fan belt, cylinder head gasket 'blown', partial mechanical seizure of engine, blocked or damaged exhaust system.

48. If engine temperature is normal, check cylinder compressions.

49. If cylinder compression readings low, add a couple of teaspoons of engine oil to each cylinder in turn, and repeat test. If readings don't improve, suspect burnt valves/seats.

50. If compression readings improve after adding oil as described, suspect worn cylinder bores, pistons and rings.

51. If compression readings are normal, checkfor mechanical problems, for example, binding brakes, slipping clutch, partially seized transmission, etc.

Engine stops suddenly.

52. Check for sudden ingress of water/snow onto ignition components, in adverse weather conditions. Sudden failure is almost always because of an ignition fault. Check for simple wiring and connection breakdowns.

Lights fail.

53. Sudden failure - check fuses.

54. If all lamps affected, check switch and main wiring feeds.

55. If not all lamps are affected, check bulbs on lamps concerned.

56. If bulbs appear to be okay, check bulb holder(s), local wiring and connections.

57. If bulb(s) blown, replace!

58. Intermittent operation, flickering or poor light output.

59. Check earth (ground) connections(s).

60. If earth(s) okay, check switch.

61. If switch okay, check wiring and connections.

Horn failure.

62. If horn does not operate, check fuse, all connections (particularly earths/grounds) and cables. Remove horn connections and check/clean. Use 12v test lamp to ascertain power getting to horn.

63. If horn will not stop(!), disconnect the horn and check for earthing of cable between button and horn unit and the wiring and contacts in the horn switch housing. **SPECIALIST SERVICE.** Horn wiring and connections are more complex than they appear at first. If necessary, have them checked by a specialist.

pump) or switch on ignition (electric pump) and fuel should issue from pump outlet.

37. If pump is okay, check for blocked fuel filter or pipe, or major leak in pipe between tank and pump, or between pump and carb.

38. If the filter is clean and the pump operates, suspect blocked carburettor jet(s) or damaged/sticking float, or incorrectly adjusted carburettor.

39. If there is petrol in the tank but none issues from the feed pipe from pump to carburettor, check that the small vent hole in the fuel filler cap is not blocked and causing a vacuum. NOTE: On some cars there is no vent hole in the filler cap. Other arrangements are made for venting the tank. There are many systems - **SPECIALIST SERVICE.**

40. If fuel is present at carburettor feed pipe, remove spark plugs and check whether wet with unburnt fuel.

41. If the spark plugs are fuel-soaked, check that the choke is operating as it should and is not jammed 'shut'. Other possibilities include float needle valve(s) sticking 'open' or leaking, float punctured, carburettor incorrectly adjusted or air filter totally blocked. Clean plugs before replacing.

42. If the spark plugs are dry, check whether the float needle valve is jammed 'shut'.

43. Check for severe air leak at inlet manifold gasket or carburettor gasket. Incorrectly set valve clearances.

Engine lacks power.

44. Engine overheating. Check oil temperature gauge (where fitted). Low oil pressure light may come on.

45. Air cleaner intake thermostat not opening/closing at the correct temperatures. Replace or free-off as necessary.

46. If thermostat okay, check oil level. BEWARE - DIPSTICK AND OIL MAY BE VERY HOT.

Fuel gauge problems.

64. Gauge reads 'empty' - check for fuel in tank!

65. If fuel is present in tank, check for earthing of wiring from tank to gauge, and for wiring disconnections.

66. Gauge permanently reads 'full', regardless of tank contents. Check wiring and connections as in '65'.

67. If wiring and connections all okay, sender unit/fuel gauge defective.

68. With wiring disconnected, check for continuity between fuel gauge terminals. Do NOT test gauge by short-circuiting to earth. Replace unit if faulty.

69. If gauge is okay, disconnect wiring from tank sender unit and check for continuity between terminal and case. Replace sender unit if faulty.

FACT FILE: EMERGENCY STARTING

Pushing or Towing

NOTE: This is not possible for vehicles with automatic transmission. Diesel engines: only attempt in warm weather or with a warm engine.

Turn off all unnecessary electrical load; switch on ignition and depress the clutch pedal. Select second or third gear; release the clutch when the car reaches a person's running speed.

Starting with Jump Leads

Safety First!
This process can be dangerous and the following instructions must be followed to the letter. Also see **Chapter One, Safety First!** *and the relevant part of* **Chapter 3** *for information on safe handling of car batteries.*

Ensure that the battery providing the jump start has the same voltage (12 volt) as the battery fitted to your car.

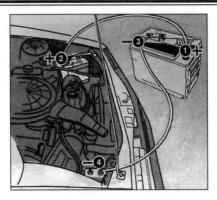

Do not lean over the battery during jump starting.

Switch off all unnecessary electrical loads and apply the hand brake. Auto. Transmission: Place gear selector in 'P'. Manual Transmission: Place gear shift lever in neutral.

Note that on some batteries and on battery connections, '+' (positive) terminals are coloured red and '-' (negative) terminals are coloured blue or black.

Run the engine of the vehicle providing the jump start (if battery fitted to vehicle).

(The following instruction numbers refer to the numbers on the drawing.)

1. Connect one end of the jump lead to the positive ('+') terminal of the battery providing the jump start.

2. Connect the other end of the same lead to the positive terminal on the car being started.

3. Connect one end of the other jump lead to the negative ('-') terminal on the 'slave' battery...

4. ...and the other end to the negative battery lead on the car, or to some bare metal in the car's engine bay.

Now try to start the car as quickly as is reasonably possible.

IT IS IMPORTANT that the leads are removed in the exact reverse sequence to that shown above. Keep hands, hair and loose clothing away from moving parts in both engine bays.

CHAPTER 7
GETTING THROUGH THE MOT

This Chapter is for owners in Britain whose vehicles need to pass the 'MoT' test. The Test was first established in 1961 by the then Ministry of Transport and it attempts to ensure that vehicles using British roads reach minimum standards of safety. Approximately 40 per cent of vehicles submitted for the test fail it, but many of these failures could be avoided by knowing what the vehicle might 'fall down on', and by taking appropriate remedial action before the test 'proper' is carried out.

It is true that the scope of the test has been considerably enlarged in the past few years, with the result that it is correspondingly more difficult to be sure that your vehicle will reach the required standards. In truth, however, a careful examination of the relevant areas, perhaps a month or so before the current certificate expires, will highlight components which require attention, and enable any obvious faults to be rectified before you take the vehicle for the test.

Getting Ahead

It is also worth noting that a vehicle can be submitted for a test up to a month before the current certificate expires - if the vehicle passes, the new certificate will be valid for one year from the day of expiry of the old one, provided that the old certificate is produced at the time of the test.

PART I: THE BACKGROUND

Keeping Up To Date

Alterations are being made to the Test on a regular basis - almost always making it tougher than it was before. It is MOST IMPORTANT that UK owners find out for themselves about any changes in the requirements that might have been made since this book was written. Your local MoT Testing Station should be able to help - if not, take your custom elsewhere! Also, non-UK owners should obtain information on the legal requirements in their own territory - and act accordingly.

Making A Good Impression

If your vehicle is muddy or particularly dirty (especially underneath) it would be worth giving it a thorough clean a day or two before carrying out the inspection so that it has ample time to dry. Do the same before the real MoT test. A clean vehicle makes a better impression on the examiner, who can refuse to test a vehicle which is particularly dirty underneath.

On the other hand, a clean vehicle makes a better impression and it will help the examiner to see what he is supposed to be examining. Generally, this will work in the owner's favour. For example, if a component or an area of underbody or chassis is particularly difficult to examine due to a build-up of oily dirt etc., and if the examiner is in doubt about its condition, he is entitled to fail that component because it was not possible for him to conclude that it reached the required standard. Had it been clean, it might well have been tested, and passed!

MoT testers do not dismantle assemblies during the test but you may wish to do so during your pretest check-up for a better view of certain wearing parts, such as the rear brake

SAFETY FIRST!
The MoT tester will follow a set procedure and we will cover the ground in a similar way, starting inside the vehicle, then continuing outside, under the bonnet, underneath the vehicle, etc. When preparing to go underneath the vehicle, do ensure that it is jacked on firm level ground and then supported on axle stands or ramps which are adequate for the task. Wheels which remain on the ground should have chocks in front of and behind them, and while the rear wheels remain on the ground, the hand brake should be firmly ON. For most repair and replacement jobs under your vehicle these normal precautions will suffice. However, the vehicle needs to be even more stable than usual when carrying out these checks. There must be no risk of it toppling off its stands while suspension and steering components are being pushed and pulled in order to test them. Read carefully Chapter 1, Safety First! and the first part of Chapter 3, Servicing Your Car for further important information on raising and supporting a vehicle above the ground.

shoes for example. See *Chapter 3, Servicing Your Car* for information on how to check the brakes.

Buying And Selling

This chapter provides a procedure for checking your vehicle's condition prior to its official MoT test. The same procedure could be equally useful to UK and non-UK owners alike when examining vehicles prior to purchase (or sale for that matter). However, it must be emphasised that the official MoT certificate should not be regarded as any guarantee of the condition of a vehicle. All it proves is that the vehicle reached the required standards, in the opinion of a particular examiner, at the time and date it was tested.

Pass The MoT!

The aim of this chapter is to explain what is actually tested on a vehicle and (if it is not obvious) how the test is done. This should enable you to identify and eliminate problems before they undermine the safety or diminish the performance of your vehicle and long before they cause the expense and inconvenience of a test failure.

Tool Box

Dismantling apart, few tools are needed for testing. A light hammer is useful for tapping panels underneath the vehicle when looking for rust. If this produces a bright metallic noise, then the area being tapped is solid metal. If the noise produced is dull, the area contains rust or filler. When tapping sills and box sections, listen also for the sound of debris (that is, rust flakes) on the inside of the panel. Use a screwdriver to prod weak parts of panels. This may produce holes of course, but if the panels have rusted to that extent, you really ought to know about it. A strong lever (such as a tyre lever) can be useful for applying the required force to suspension joints etc. when assessing whether there is any wear in them.

You will need an assistant to operate controls and perhaps to wobble the road wheels while you inspect components under the vehicle.

Age Related Checks

Two more brief explanations are required before you start your informal test. Firstly, the age of the vehicle determines exactly which lights, seat belts and other items it should have. Frequently in the next few pages you will come across the phrase "Cars first used ..." followed by a date. A vehicle's "first used" date is either its date of first registration, or the date six months after it was manufactured, whichever was earlier. Or, if the vehicle was originally used without being registered (such as a vehicle which has been imported to the U.K. or an ex-H.M. Forces model, etc.) the "first used" date is the date of manufacture.

Rust And Load Bearing Areas

Secondly, there must not be excessive rust, serious distortion or any fractures affecting certain prescribed areas of the bodywork. These prescribed areas are load-bearing parts of the bodywork within 30 cm (12 in.) of anchorages or mounting points associated with testable items such as seat belts, brake pedal assemblies, master cylinders, servos, suspension and

steering components and also body mountings. Keep this rule in mind while inspecting the vehicle, but remember also that even if such damage occurs outside a prescribed area, it can cause failure of the test. Failure will occur if the damage is judged to reduce the continuity or strength of a main load-bearing part of the bodywork sufficiently to have an adverse effect on the braking or steering.

The following notes are necessarily abbreviated, and are for assistance only. They are not a definitive guide to all the MoT regulations. It is also worth mentioning that the varying degrees of discretion of individual MoT testers can mean that there are variations between the standards as applied. However, the following points should help to make you aware of the aspects which will be examined. Now, if you have your clipboard, checklist and pencil handy, let's make a start...

The 'Easy' Bits

Checking these items is straightforward and should not take more than a few minutes - and could avoid an embarrassingly simple failure...

Lights

Within the scope of the test are headlights, side and tail lights, brake lights, direction indicators, and number plate lights (plus rear fog lights on all cars first used on or after 1 April, 1980, and any earlier cars subsequently so equipped, and also hazard warning lights on any vehicle so fitted). All must operate, must be clean and not significantly damaged; flickering is also not permitted. The switches should also all work properly. Pairs of lights should give approximately the same intensity of light output, and operation of one set of lights should not affect the working of another - such trouble is usually due to bad earthing.

Front fog and spot lights are not part of the MoT test (although their use is covered by *Construction and Use* regulations so that, for instance, spot lights should go out when headlights are turned off main beam) and won't be tested, provided they're not a physical hazard. Rear fog lights are part of the Test however. See later in this Chapter for details.

Indicators should flash at between 60 and 120 times per minute. 'Rev' the engine to encourage them, if a little slow (although the examiner might not let you get away with it!) Otherwise, renew the (inexpensive) flasher unit and check all wiring and earth connections.

Interior 'tell-tale' lights, such as for indicators, rear fog lights and hazard warning lights should all operate in unison with their respective exterior lights.

Headlight aim must be correct - in particular, the lights should not dazzle other road users. An approximate guide can be obtained by shining the lights against a vertical wall, but final adjustment may be necessary by reference to the beam checking machine at the MoT station. Most testers will be happy to make slight adjustments where necessary but only if the adjusters work. Make sure before you take the vehicle in that they are not seized solid!

Reflectors must be unbroken, clean, and not obscured - for example, by stickers.

Wheels And Tyres

Check the wheels for loose nuts, cracks, and damaged rims. Missing wheel nuts or studs are also failure points, naturally enough!

There is no excuse for running on illegal tyres. The legal requirement is that there must be at least 1.6 mm of tread depth remaining, over the 'central' three-quarters of the width of the tyre all the way around. From this it can be deduced that there is no legal requirement to have 1.6 mm (1/16 in.) of tread on the 'shoulders' of the tyre, but in practice, most MoT stations will be reluctant to pass a tyre in this condition. In any case, for optimum safety - especially 'wet grip' - you would be well advised to change tyres when they wear down to around 3 mm (1/8 in.) or so depth of remaining tread.

Visible 'tread wear indicator bars', found approximately every nine inches around the tread of the tyre, are highlighted when the tread reaches the critical 1.6 mm point.

Tyres should not show signs of cuts or bulges, rubbing on the bodywork or running gear, and the valves should be in sound condition, and correctly aligned.

Old-fashioned cross-ply and radial-ply tyre types must not be mixed on the same axle, and if pairs of cross-ply and radial-ply tyres are fitted, the radials must be on the rear axle.

Windscreen

The screen must not be damaged (by cracks, chips, etc.) or obscured so that the driver does not have a clear view of the road. Permissible size of damage points depends on where they occur. Within an area 290 mm (nearly 12 in.) wide, ahead of the driver, and up to the top of the wiper arc, any damage must be confined within a circle less than 10 mm (approx. 0.4 in.) in diameter. This is increased to 40 mm (just over 1.5 in.) for damage within the rest of the screen area swept by the wipers.

Washers And Wipers

The wipers must clear an area big enough to give the driver a clear view forwards and to the side of the vehicle. The wiper blades must be securely attached and sound, with no cracks or 'missing' sections. The wiper switch should also work properly. The screen washers must supply the screen with sufficient liquid to keep it clean, in conjunction with the use of the wipers.

Mirrors

Your vehicle must have at least two, one of which must be on the driver's side. The mirrors must be visible from the driver's seat, and not be damaged or obscured so that the view to the rear is affected. Therefore cracks, chips and discolouration can mean failure.

Horn

The horn must emit a uniform note which is loud enough to give adequate warning of approach, and the switch must operate correctly. Multi-tone horns playing 'in sequence' are not permitted, but two tones sounding together are fine.

Seat Security

The seats must be securely mounted, and the sub-frames should be sound.

Seat Belts

Seat belts must be in good condition (i.e. not frayed or otherwise damaged), and the buckles and catches should also operate correctly. Inertia reel types, where fitted, should retract properly.

Belt mountings must be secure, with no structural damage or corrosion within 30 cm (12 in.) of them.

Number (Registration) Plates

Both front and rear number plates must be present, and in good condition, with no breaks or missing numbers or letters. The plates must not be obscured, and the digits must not be repositioned (to form names, for instance).

Vehicle Identification Numbers (VIN)

Vehicles first used on or after 1 August, 1980 have to have a clearly displayed VIN - Vehicle Identification Number (or old-fashioned 'chassis numbers' for older cars) which is plainly legible. See *Chapter 2, Buying Guide* for the correct location on your vehicle.

Exhaust System

The entire system must be present, properly mounted, free of leaks and should not be noisy - which can happen when the internal baffles fail. 'Proper' repairs by welding, or exhaust cement, or bandage are acceptable, as long as no gas leaks are evident. Then again, common sense, if not the MoT, dictates that exhaust bandage should only be a very short-term emergency measure. For safety's sake, fit a new exhaust if yours is reduced to this!

PART II: THE CHECKLIST

You've checked the easy bits - now it's time for the detail! Some of the 'easy bits' referred to above are included here, but this is intended as a more complete check list to give your vehicle the best possible chance of gaining a First Class Honours, MoT Pass!

Inside The Vehicle

☐ 1. The steering wheel should be examined for cracks and for damage which might interfere with its use, or injure the driver's hands. It should also be pushed and pulled along the column axis, and also up and down, at 90 degrees to it. This will highlight any deficiencies in the wheel and upper column mounting/bearing, and also any excessive end float, and movement between the column shaft and the wheel. Look, too, for movement in the steering column couplings and fasteners (including the universal joint if applicable), and visually check their condition and security. They must be sound, and properly tightened.

In the case of cars (the majority) with steering racks, rotate the steering wheel in both directions to test for free play at the wheel rim - this shouldn't exceed approximately 13 mm. (0.5 in.), assuming a 380 mm. (15 in.) diameter steering wheel.

In the case of the smaller number of cars with steering boxes, free play at the wheel rim shouldn't exceed approximately 75 mm (3.0 in.), assuming a 380 mm (15 in.) diameter steering wheel.

In both cases where the steering wheel is larger or smaller the amount of permissible free play should be raised or lowered accordingly.

☐ 2. Check that the switches for headlights, sidelights, rear fog lights direction indicators, hazard warning lights, wipers, washers and horn, appear to be in good working order and check that the tell-tale lights or audible warnings are working where applicable.

☐ 3. Make sure that the windscreen wipers operate effectively with blades that are secure and in good condition. The windscreen washer should provide sufficient liquid to clear the screen in conjunction with the wipers.

☐ 4. Check for windscreen damage, especially in the area swept by the wipers. From the MoT tester's point of view, Zone A is part of this area, 290 mm (11.5 in.) wide and centred on the centre of the steering wheel. Damage to the screen within this area should be capable of fitting into a 10 mm (approx. 0.4 in.) diameter circle and the cumulative effect of more minor damage should not seriously restrict the driver's view. Windscreen stickers or other obstructions should not encroach more than 10 mm (approx 0.4 in.) into this area. In the remainder of the swept area the maximum diameter of damage or degree of encroachment by obstructions is 40 mm (approx. 1.6 in.) and there is no ruling regarding cumulative

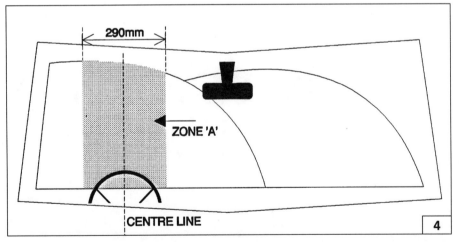

290mm

ZONE 'A'

CENTRE LINE

4

damage. Specialist windscreen companies can often repair a cracked screen for a lot less than the cost of replacement. Moreover, the cost of repair is often covered by comprehensive insurance policies. DIY repair kits are also available.

☐ 5. The horn control should be present, secure and readily accessible to the driver, and the horn should be loud enough to be heard by other road users. Gongs, bells and sirens are not permitted (except as part of an anti-theft device) and

multi-tone horns (which alternate between two or more notes) are not permitted at all. On cars first used after 1 August 1973, the horn should produce a constant, continuous or uniform note which is neither harsh nor grating.

☐ 6. There must be one exterior mirror on the driver's side of the vehicle and one other mirror - either an exterior mirror fitted to the passenger's side or an interior mirror. The required mirrors should be secure and in good condition.

☐ 7. Check that the hand brake operates effectively without coming to the end of its working travel. The lever and its mechanism must be complete, securely mounted, unobstructed in its travel and in a sufficiently good condition to remain firmly in the "On" position even when knocked from side to side. The 30 cm rule on bodywork corrosion applies in the vicinity of the hand brake lever mounting.

☐ 8. The foot brake pedal assembly should be complete, unobstructed, and in a good working condition, including the pedal rubber (which should not have been worn smooth). There should be no excessive movement of the pedal at right angles to its normal direction. When fully depressed, the pedal should not be at the end of its travel. The pedal should not feel spongy (indicating air in the hydraulic system), nor should it tend to creep downwards while held under pressure (which indicates an internal hydraulic leak).

☐ 9. Seats must be secure on their mountings and seat backs must be capable of being locked in the upright position.

☐ 10. The law requires all models to be fitted with seatbelts for the driver and front passenger. These have to be three-point lap and diagonal belts. Rear seat belts are a requirement for vehicles first used after 31 March 1987 with three anchorage points for the 'outer' passengers, and at least a lap belt only for the centre passenger position. Examine seat belt webbing and fittings to make sure that all are in good condition and that anchorages are firmly attached to the vehicle's structure. Locking mechanisms should be capable of remaining locked, and of being released if required, when under load. Flexible buckle stalks (if fitted) should be free of corrosion, broken cable strands or other weaknesses. Note that any belts fitted which are not part of a legal requirements may be examined by the tester but will not form part of the official test.

☐ 11. On inertia reel belts, check that on retracting the belts, the webbing winds into the retracting unit automatically, albeit with some manual assistance to start with.

☐ 12. Note the point raised earlier regarding corrosion around seat belt anchorage points. The MoT tester will not carry out any dismantling here, but he will examine floor mounted anchorage points from underneath the vehicle if that is possible.

☐ 13. Before getting out of the vehicle, make sure that both doors can be opened from the inside.

Outside The Vehicle

☐ 14. Before closing the driver's door, check the condition of the inner sill. Usually the MoT tester will do this by applying finger or thumb pressure to various parts of the panel while the floor covering remains in place. For your own peace of mind, look beneath the sill covering, taking great care not to tear any covering. Then close the driver's door and make sure that it latches securely and repeat these checks on the nearside inner sill and door.

Now check all of the lights, front and rear, (and the number plate lights) while your assistant operates the light switches.

☐ 15. As we said earlier, you can carry out a rough and ready check on headlight alignment for yourself, although it will certainly not be as accurate as having it done for you at the MoT testing station. Drive your vehicle near to a wall, as shown. Check that your tyres are correctly inflated and the vehicle is on level ground.

Draw on the wall, with chalk:
• a horizontal line about 2 metres long, and at same height as centre of headlight lenses.
• two vertical lines about 1 metre long, each forming a cross with the horizontal line and the same distance apart as the headlight centres.
• another vertical line to form a cross on the horizontal line, midway between the others.

Now position your vehicle so that:
• it faces the wall squarely, and its centre line is in line with centre line marked on the wall.
• the steering is straight.
• headlight lenses are 5.0 metres (16 ft.) from the wall.

Switch on the headlights' 'main' and 'dipped' beams in turn and measure their centre points. You will be able to judge any major discrepancies in intensity and aim prior to having the beams properly set by a garage with beam measuring equipment.

Headlights should be complete, clean, securely mounted, in good working order and not adversely affected by the operation of another lamp, and these basic requirements affect all the lights listed below. Headlights must dip as a pair from a single switch. Their aim must be correctly adjusted and they should not be affected (even to the extent of flickering) when lightly tapped by hand. Each headlight should match its partner in terms of size, colour and intensity of light, and can be white or yellow.

☐ 16. Side lights should show white light to the front and red light to the rear. Lenses should not be broken, cracked or incomplete. Stop lights must be red, of course.

☐ 17. Check your indicators, doing what the MoT tester will do: turn on side lights and apply the brake lights while ensuring that the indicators still work properly, and that none of the lights interfere with each other, causing dimness or intermittent failure. Check side repeater lights, too.

☐ 18. Vehicles first used before 1 April 1986 do not have to have a hazard warning device, but if one is fitted, it must be tested, and it must operate with the ignition switch either on or off. The lights should flash 60-120 times per minute, and indicators must operate independently of any other lights.

☐ 19. There must be two red rear reflectors - always fitted by the manufacturers, of course! - which are clean and are securely and symmetrically fitted to the vehicle.

☐ 20. Your vehicle must have at least one rear fog light fitted to the centre or offside of the vehicle. If there are two, they must be spaced an equal distance from the centre. It must comply with the basic requirements (listed under headlights) and emit a steady red light. Its tell-tale light, inside the vehicle, must work to inform the driver that it is switched on.

☐ 21. There must be registration number plates at the front and rear of the vehicle and both must be clean, secure, complete and unobscured. Letters and figures must be correctly formed and correctly spaced and not likely to be misread due to an uncovered securing bolt or whatever. The year letter counts as a figure. The space between letters and figures must be at least twice that between adjacent letters or figures.

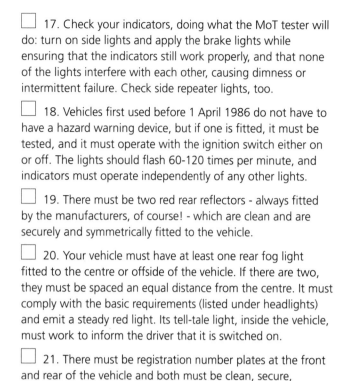

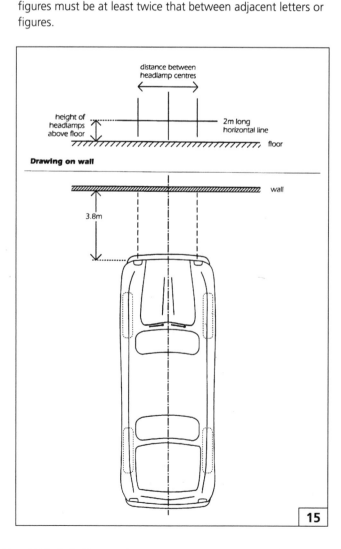

□ 22. Number plate lights must be present, working, and must not flicker when tapped by hand, just as for other lights. Where more than one light or bulb was fitted as original equipment, all must be working.

Wheels And Tyres

The MoT tester will examine tyres and wheels while walking around the vehicle and again when he is underneath it.

□ 23. Front tyres should match each other and rear tyres should match each other, both sets matching in terms of size, aspect ratio and type of structure. For example, you must never fit tyres of different sizes or types, such as cross-ply or radial, on the same 'axle' - both front wheels counting as 'on the same axle' in this context. If cross-ply or bias belted tyres are fitted to the rear of the car, you must not fit radial-ply tyres to the front. If cross-ply tyres are fitted to the rear, bias belted tyres should not be fitted to the front. (We recommend that you do not mix tyre types anywhere on the car.)

□ 24. Failure of the test can be caused by a cut, lump, tear or bulge in a tyre, exposed ply or cord, a badly seated tyre, a re-cut tyre, a tyre fouling part of the vehicle, or a seriously damaged or misaligned valve stem which could cause sudden deflation of the tyre. To pass the test, the grooves of the tread pattern must be at least 1.6 mm deep throughout a continuous band comprising the central three-quarters of the breadth of tread, and round the entire outer circumference of the tyre.

We are grateful to Dunlop/SP Tyres for the photographs and information in this section.

□ 24A. Modern tyres have tread wear indicators built into the tread groves (usually about eight of them spread equidistantly around the circumference). These appear as continuous bars running across the tread when the original pattern depth has worn down to 1.6 mm. There will be a distinct reduction in wet grip well before the tread wear indicators start to show, and you should replace tyres before they get to this stage, even though this is the legal minimum in the UK.

□ 24B. Lumps and bulges in the tyre wall usually arise from accidental damage or even because of faults in the tyre construction. You should run your hand all the way around the side wall of the tyre, with the vehicle either jacked off the ground, or moving the vehicle half a wheels revolution, so that you can check the part of the tyre that was previously resting on the ground. Since you can't easily check the insides of the tyres in day-to-day use, it is even more important that you spend time carefully checking the inside of each tyre - the MoT tester will certainly do so! Tyres with bulges in them must be scrapped and replaced with new, since they can fail suddenly, causing your vehicle to lose control.

□ 24C. Abrasion of the tyre side wall can take place either in conjunction with bulging, or by itself, and this invariably results from an impact, such as the tyre striking the edge of a kerb or a pothole in the road. Once again, the tyre may be at imminent risk of failure and you should take advice from a tyre specialist on whether the abrasion is just superficial, or whether the tyre will need replacement.

NEW TYRE TWI ILLEGAL TYRE 24A

24D. All tyres will suffer progressively from cracking, albeit in most cases superficially, due to the effects of sunlight. If old age has caused the tyres on your vehicle to degrade to this extent, replace them.

24E. If the outer edges of the tread are worn noticeably more than the centre, the tyres have been run under inflated which not only ruins tyres, but causes worse fuel consumption, dangerous handling and is, of course, illegal.

Over-inflation causes the centre part of the tyre to wear more quickly than the outer edges. This is also illegal but in addition, it causes the steering and grip to suffer and the tyre becomes more susceptible to concussion damage.

24F. Incorrect wheel alignment causes one side of the tyre to wear more severely than the other. If your vehicle should hit a kerb or large pothole, it is worthwhile having the wheel alignment checked by a tyre specialist since this costs considerably less than new front tyres!

25. Road wheels must be secure and must not be badly damaged, distorted or cracked, or have badly distorted bead rims (perhaps due to "kerbing"), or loose or missing wheel nuts, studs or bolts.

26. Check the bodywork for any sharp edges or projections, caused by corrosion or damage, which could prove dangerous to other road users, including pedestrians.

27. Check that the fuel cap fastens securely and that its sealing washer is neither torn nor deteriorated, or its mounting flange damaged sufficiently to allow fuel to escape (for example, while the vehicle is cornering).

Under The Bonnet

28. The vehicle should have a Vehicle Identification Number fitted to the bodywork. This can be on a plate secured to the vehicle or, etched or stamped on the bodywork. See *Chapter 2, Buying Guide* for more information.

29. Check the steering rack or box for security by asking your assistant to turn the steering wheel from side to side (with the road wheels on the ground) while you watch what happens under the bonnet. Then, check for free play in the steering assembly as a whole. This is done by turning the steering wheel from side to side as far as possible without moving the road wheels - and measuring how far the steering wheel can be moved in this way. More than 75 mm (approx. 3 in.) of free play, on a steering box system, or 13 mm (approx. 0.5 in.), on a steering rack, at the perimeter of the steering wheel, due to wear in the steering components, is sufficient grounds for a test failure. Note that the free play is based on a steering wheel diameter of 380 mm (approx 15 in) and will be less for smaller steering wheels - which all of them virtually are! Also check for the presence and security of retaining and locking devices in the steering column assembly.

30. While peering under the bonnet, check that hydraulic master cylinders and reservoirs are securely mounted and not severely corroded or otherwise damaged. Ensure that the caps are present, that fluid levels are satisfactory and that there are no fluid leaks.

31. Also check that the brake servo is securely mounted and not damaged or corroded to an extent that would impair its operation. Vacuum pipes should be sound, that is, free from kinks, splits and excessive chafing and not collapsed internally.

32. Still under the bonnet have a thorough search for evidence of excessive corrosion, severe distortion or fracture in any load bearing panelling within 30 cm (12 in.) of important mounting points such as the master cylinder/servo mounting, front suspension mountings etc.

Under The Vehicle - Front End

☐ **33. SAFETY FIRST! On some occasions there is no alternative but for your assistant to sit in the vehicle whilst you go beneath. Therefore: 1) Place ramps as well as axle stands beneath the vehicle's structure so that it cannot fall. 2) Don't allow your assistant to move vigorously or get in or out of the vehicle while you are beneath it. If either of these are problematical, DON'T CARRY OUT CHECK 34 - leave it to your garage.**

☐ 34. Have an assistant turn the steering wheel from side to side while you watch for movement in the steering mechanism. Make sure that the rack or box mountings are secure, that the ball joints show no signs of wear and that the ball joint dust covers are in sound condition. Ensure that all split pins, locking nuts and so on are in place and correctly fastened, throughout the steering and suspension systems.

☐ 35. With each wheel raised in turn, spin the wheel listening for roughness in the bearings. There must be none.

☐ 36. Under the vehicle, check the condition of the front springs. Wearing goggles, use a stuff brush to clean off the mud and other debris so that you don't miss a hidden 'crack'. Make sure that all suspension mountings are sound.

☐ 37. Inspect the front shock absorbers. Their upper shrouds (outer casing) tend to rust. Any sign of leaks will cause failure of the test - look for weeping hydraulic fluid just below the lower edge of the upper shroud. Take a firm grip on the upper and lower shroud in turn with both hands and try to twist the damper to check for deterioration in the top and bottom mounting bushes.

☐ 38. With all four wheels on the ground, push down firmly a couple of times on each front wing of the vehicle, then let go at the bottom of the stroke. The vehicle should return to approximately its original level within two or three strokes. Continuing oscillations will earn your vehicle a 'failure' ticket for worn front shockers!

Under The Vehicle - Rear Suspension

☐ 39. Check the operation of the rear shock absorbers in the same way as the front (Check 38).

☐ 40. Check the rear wheel bearings as described in check 35.

☐ 41. Check the condition of the rear springs and suspension components as described in check 36.

☐ 42. Check the condition of the rear shock absorbers as described in check 37.

Braking System

☐ 43. The MoT brake test is carried out on a special 'rolling road' set-up, which measures the efficiency in terms of percentage. For the foot brake, the examiner is looking for 50 per cent; the hand brake must measure 25 per cent. Frankly, without a rolling road of your own, there is little that you can do to verify whether or not your vehicle will come up to the required figures. What you can do, though, is carry out an entire check of the brake system, which will also cover all other aspects the examiner will be checking, and be as sure as you can that the system is working efficiently.

IMPORTANT! See *Chapter 3, Servicing Your Car* for important information, including *SAFETY FIRST!* information before working on your vehicle's brakes.

☐ 44. The MoT examiner will not dismantle any part of the system, but you can do so. So, take off each front wheel in turn, and examine as follows:

Disc Brakes

Check the front brake discs themselves, looking for excessive grooving or crazing, the calliper pistons/dust seals (looking for signs of fluid leakage and deterioration of the seals), and the brake pads - ideally, replace them if less than approximately 3mm (1/8th in.) friction material remains on each pad - but check the recommendations in *Chapter 3*.

Drum Brakes

Remove each brake drum and check the condition of the linings (renew if worn down to anywhere near the rivet heads), the brake drum (watch for cracking, ovality and serious scoring, etc.) and the wheel cylinders. Check the cylinder's dust covers to see if they contain brake fluid. If so, or if it is obvious that the cylinder(s) have been leaking, replace them or - ONLY if the cylinder bore is in perfect condition - fit a new seal kit.

☐ 45. Ensure that the drum brake adjusters (where fitted) are free to rotate (i.e. not seized!). If they are stuck fast, apply a little penetrating oil (but if possible, only from behind the backplate; if you have to work inside the brake drum, take great care to avoid the risk of getting oil on the brake shoes), and gently work the adjuster backwards and forwards with a brake adjuster spanner. Eventually the adjusters should free and a little brake grease can be applied to the threads to keep them in this condition. Now rotate the adjuster until the brake shoes contact the drum (preventing the road wheel from turning), then reverse the adjustment just enough to allow the wheel to turn.

☐ 46. A similar procedure can be applied to the handbrake adjustment. Check that the handbrake applies the brakes fully, well before it reaches the end of its potential range of movement. Ensure that the handbrake lever remains locked in the 'on' position when fully applied, even if the lever is knocked sideways.

☐ 47. Closely check the state of ALL visible hydraulic pipework. If any section of the steel tubing shows signs of corrosion, replace it, for safety as well as to gain an MoT pass. Look too for leakage of fluid around pipe joints, and from the master cylinder. The fluid level in the master cylinder reservoir must also be at its correct level - if not, find out why and rectify the problem! At the front and rear of the vehicle, bend the flexible hydraulic pipes (by hand) near each end of each pipe, checking for signs of cracking. If any is evident, or if the pipes have been chafing on the tyres, wheels, steering or suspension components, replace them with new items, rerouting them to avoid future problems. Note also that where the manufacturers fitted a clip to secure a piece of pipe, then it must be present and the pipe must be secured by it.

□ 48. Have an assistant press down hard on the brake pedal while you check all flexible pipes for bulges. As an additional check, firmly apply the foot brake and hold the pedal down for a few minutes. It should not slowly sink to the floor (if it does, you have a hydraulic system problem). Press and release the pedal a few times - it should not feel 'spongy' (due to the presence of air in the system). Now check the operation of the brake servo by starting the engine while the brake pedal is being held down. If all is well, as the vacuum servo starts to work, the pedal should move a short distance towards the floor. Check the condition of the servo unit and its hoses - all MUST be sound. If there is the risk of any problems with the braking system's hydraulics, have a qualified mechanic check it over before using the vehicle.

□ 49. A test drive should reveal obvious faults (such as pulling to one side, due to a seized calliper piston, for example), but otherwise all will be revealed on the rollers at the MoT station...

Bodywork Structure

A structurally deficient vehicle is a dangerous vehicle, and rust can affect many important areas, including the sills, any 'outriggers' and the floorpan. Examine these areas carefully.

□ 50. Essentially, fractures, cracks or serious corrosion in any load bearing panel or member (to the extent that the affected sections are weakened) need to be dealt with. In addition, failure will result from any deficiencies in the structural metalwork within 30 cm (12 in.) of the seat belt mountings, and also the steering and suspension component attachment points. Repairs made to any structural areas must be carried out by 'continuous' seam welding, and the repair should restore the affected section to at least its original strength.

□ 51. The MoT examiner will be looking for metal which gives way under squeezing pressure between finger and thumb, and will use his wicked little 'Corrosion Assessment Tool' (i.e. a plastic-headed tool known as the 'toffee hammer'!), which in theory at least should be used for detecting rust by lightly tapping the surface. If scraping the surface of the metal shows weakness beneath, the vehicle will fail.

□ 52. Note that the security of doors and other openings must also be assessed, including the hinges, locks and catches. Corrosion damage or other weakness in the vicinity of these

items can mean failure. All doors must latch securely. It must be possible to open both front doors from inside and outside the vehicle and rear doors from the outside only.

Exterior Bodywork

□ 53. Look out for surface rust, or accident damage, on the exterior bodywork, which leaves sharp/jagged edges and which may be liable to cause injury. Ideally, repairs should be carried out by welding in new metal, but for non-structural areas, riveting a plate over a hole, bridging the gap with glass fibre/body filler or even taping over the gap can be legally acceptable, at least as far as the MoT test is concerned.

Fuel System

□ 54. Another recent extension of the regulations brings the whole of the fuel system under scrutiny, from the tank to the engine. The system should be examined with and without the engine running, and there must be no leaks from any of the components. The tank must be securely mounted, and the filler cap must fit properly - 'temporary' caps are not permitted.

Emissions

□ 55. In almost every case, a proper 'engine tune' will help to ensure that your vehicle is running at optimum efficiency, and there should be no difficulty in passing the test, unless your engine or its ancillaries are well worn.

All petrol engines are subject to the 'visual smoke emission' test. The engine must be fully warmed up, allowed to idle, then revved slightly. If smoke emitted is regarded by the examiner as being 'excessive', the vehicle will fail. Often smoke emitted during this test is as a result of worn valve stem seals, allowing oil into the combustion chambers during tickover, to be blown out of the exhaust as 'blue smoke' when the engine is revved. In practice, attitudes vary widely between MoT stations on this aspect of the test.

□ 56. For diesel-engined vehicles a 'smoke' test also applies. Again, the engine must be fully warmed up, and allowed to idle, before being revved to around 2,500 rpm for 20 seconds (to 'purge' the system). If dense blue or black smoke is emitted for more than five seconds, the vehicle will fail. In addition, the exhaust smoke is tested. Problems will require **SPECIALIST SERVICE.**

GETTING THROUGH THE MOT

FACT FILE: VEHICLE EMISSIONS

PETROL ENGINED VEHICLES WITHOUT CATALYTIC CONVERTERS

Vehicles first used before 1 August 1973
- visual smoke check only.

Vehicles first used between 1 August 1973 and 31 July 1986
- 4.5% carbon monoxide and 1,200 parts per million, unburned hydrocarbons.

Vehicles first used between 1 August 1986 and 31 July 1992
- 3.5% carbon monoxide and 1,200 parts per million, unburned hydrocarbons.

FACT FILE: SU CARBURETTORS

Normally, if the CO reading is within limits, the hydrocarbon emissions will be acceptable. But, unfortunately, some cars fitted with SU carburettors, including Metros, give excessive hydrocarbon percentage readings when checked with the engine idling - EVEN WITH A NEW CARBURETTOR. Rover introduced a transmission controlled spark advance system to counteract this but many Metros without it were 'failing' the test and, in some cases, their owners were persuaded to spend large sums of money on replacement carburettors they didn't need.

Therefore a little known, but vitally important, exemption was introduced by the Vehicle Inspectorate Executive Agency in the form of Special Notice 18/19, Section 2. Copies were circulated to all MOT testing stations, but an unofficial survey by one of the car clubs revealed that many examiners were either unaware of, or had forgotten, this exemption. The Special Notice acknowledges that some vehicles, including some Metros, were unable to meet the hydrocarbon limit, even when new. If such vehicles meet the CO requirements at normal idling speed, but fail the hydrocarbon test at the same speed, the hydrocarbon test should be repeated at an engine speed of 2,000 rpm, using only the throttle to increase the engine speed. If the hydrocarbon reading is then 1,200 ppm or less, the car will pass. So, if you have difficulties in this respect, politely show the examiner this book and quote SN 18/19 Section 2.

The Rover Metro, introduced in 1990, looked similar to its predecessor, but had new bodywork, suspension, interior and engine. It's not covered by this book.
(Illustration, courtesy Rover Group Ltd)

CHAPTER 8 - FACTS & FIGURES

This Chapter serves two main purposes. In *Part I,* we aim to provide you with a guide to all the major production changes that have taken place, and second, we supply the 'Facts & Figures' you will need when servicing your car. In fact, *Part II* of this chapter, *Capacities and Settings,* will make essential reading when you come to carrying out servicing, since you will then need to know things like the correct spark plug gap, torque settings and a whole host of other adjustments and measurements.

PART I - MAJOR MILESTONES

Please note that there have been dozens of 'special models' of Metro produced over the years, some of them in very small numbers. It simply isn't possible to list them all.

Oct. 1980 Metro range launched in the UK. 1.0 litre Basic, L and HLE ('economy') with 998cc engines, 1.3 litre S and HLS with 1275cc 'A Plus' engines. Basic 1.0 available with low compression (8.3 to 1) engine to special order. 1.0 HLE has high compression engine and higher gearing. All models have four-speed manual gearboxes, independent Hydragas suspension, front disc brakes and rear drums with servo assistance on 1.3 models.

Jan. 1981 1275cc L model available for fleet use only.

Jul. 1981 1.3 automatic launched.

Feb. 1982 1.0 City launched, similar to 1.0 L but with basic equipment and trim.

Apr. 1982 1.3 Vanden Plas launched, similar to 1.3 HLS but with luxury equipment.

May 1982 MG Metro launched, developed from 1.3 S but with uprated 72 bhp engine and modified clutch. Standard features include rear spoiler, alloy wheels and tinted glass.

Sep. 1982 1.3 L and HL models with changed interior trim and equipment. Metro Van introduced with 998cc or 1275cc engines and 250 kg. payload.

Aug. 1983 Metro 310 Van with 310 kg. payload.

Oct. 1982 MG Metro Turbo launched with turbocharged 1275cc engine, revised suspension, ventilated front discs, alloy wheels with low profile tyres, front air dam and bronze tinted glass.

Jan. 1983 1.3 HLE ('economy') launched and 1.0 HLE engine fitted to 1.0 Base and L models.

Jan. 1984 Metro City becomes new 1.0 'base' model.

Oct. 1984 5-door 1.0 City X, 1.0 L, 1.3 L, 1.3 HLE and 1.3 Vanden Plas models launched, based on 3-door models but with restyled bonnet and grille, larger fuel tank, reversing lights, reclining front seats and many other interior trim changes. All (manual) clutches now cable operated. Manual gearbox Vanden Plas models have uprated 72 bhp engine, automatic versions have 62 bhp engine.

Feb. 1986 5-door 1.3 City X launched along with Mayfair in place of HLE.

May. 1987 1.3 City 3-door automatic launched.

Jun. 1987 All models given extra soundproofing and 'single key' door locking and ignition. 'Austin' name dropped.

Oct. 1988 1.3 Sport launched with 73 bhp 1275cc MG engine and fixtures but without the MG badge. Metro VDP and Auto. models discontinued.

Sept. 1989 City model renamed Clubman, with sunroof. Metro Turbo production ends.

Sept. 1990 Austin-type Metro models (cars) discontinued and replaced by Rover Metro with new, although similar looking bodywork, and an all-new K-series engine.

Apr. 1991 Metro Vans discontinued, although new stock was still available into 1992.

The easiest way to spot a 'new' Metro (from 1990-on) at-a-glance, is by the radiator grille - or rather, the lack of an obvious one! In 1995 the Metro name was dropped and the cars became known as the 100-series. (Illustration, courtesy Rover Group Ltd)

PART II - CAPACITIES AND SETTINGS

Maintenance data and settings

Engine, all models

Number of cylinders   4

Engine code starting 85H
Bore 62.94 mm
Stroke 68.25 mm
Capacity 848cc

Engine code starting 99H
Bore 64.59 mm
Stroke 76.20 mm
Capacity 998cc

Engine code starting 12H
Bore 70.61 mm
Stroke 81.28 mm
Capacity 1,275cc

All models
Firing order   1-3-4-2 (No. 1 at water pump end of engine)

Engines using four-star leaded petrol
Valve clearance (cold)   Inlet & Exhaust 0.012 in (0.30 mm)
Except MG Turbo Inlet 0.012 - 0.014 (0.030 - 0.035 mm)
Exhaust 0.014 - 0.016 (.035 - .040 mm)

(For valve clearances, engines using unleaded petrol - see later)

Exhaust gas CO at idling 1.5 - 3.5%

998cc engines with code starting 99H, all models (except unleaded petrol spec.) 1982 - 1989 unless stated
Idle speed 650 - 750 rpm
Fast idle speed 1,100 - 1,300 rpm
Ignition timing @ 1,500 rpm vacuum disconnected: 15 degrees BTDC (Before Top Dead Centre)
Except engines starting with 99HB90P, 99HB91P, 99HB92P, 99HB93P, 99HD27P, 99HD28P, 99HD29P, 99HD27, 99HD29, 99HD30, 99HD31, in which cases:
Ignition timing @ 1,500 rpm vacuum disconnected: 5 to 7 degrees BTDC

1.0 saloons and vans with unleaded petrol 95 RON specification and engine codes starting 99H E38 and 99H E39.
Idle speed 800 - 900 rpm
Fast idle speed 1,050 - 1,200 rpm
Valve clearance 0.011 - 0.013 in (0.28 - 0.33 mm)
Ignition timing @ 1,500 rpm, vacuum disconnected:
Engines starting 99H E38, 99H E39: 15 degrees BTDC
Engines starting with 99H E35, 99H E67, 99H E68, 99H E69, 99H E70, 99H E76, 99H E94:   4 - 6 degrees BTDC

1,275cc engines with code starting 12H, all models (Except unleaded petrol spec.) 1982 - 1989 Unless stated otherwise
Idle speed 750 - 850 rpm
Fast idle speed 1,000 - 1,200 rpm
Valve clearance 0.012 in (0.030 mm)
Ignition timing @ 1,500 rpm, vacuum disconnected:
11 degrees BTDC
Except
Ignition timing @ 1,500 rpm, vacuum disconnected:
MG 1300 & Vanden Plas (Europe), 1982-on: 10 degrees BTDC
MG Metro Turbo 1982-on: 7 degrees BTDC

1.3 HLE, 1983-on: 9 degrees BTDC
1.3 litre 10.3 : 1 compression engines starting with 12HA06P,
1984-on: 7 degrees BTDC
1.3 litre 9.6 : 1 compression engines starting with
12H9O7P, 1984-on: 15 degrees BTDC
1.3 litre 8.0 : 1 compression engines starting with
12HAO22AA, 1984-on: 13 degrees BTDC
1.3, litre, 1985-on:, starting with 12HA73AA, 12HA84AA,
12HB37AA, 12HC17AA, 12HC18AA, 12HC19AA, 12HD18,
12HD19,12HD19AA, 12HD20, and 12HD20AA:
13 degrees BTDC
1.3 litre, 1985-on:, starting with 12HA74AA, 12HA79AA,
12HC12AA, 12HC13AA: 11 degrees BTDC
1.3 litre, 1985-on:, starting with 12HA60AA, 12HA61AA,
12HA62HA, 12HA71AA, 12HA72AA, 12HA80AA, 12HA86AA,
12HA87AA, 12HB09AA, 12HB22AA, 12HB36AA, 12HC01AA,
12HC02AA, 12HC03AA, 12HC04AA, 12HC05AA, 12HC06AA,
12HC07AA, 12HC08AA, 12HC09AA, 12HC10AA, 12HC11AA,
12HD14,12HD14AA, 12HD09,12HD10, 12HD11, 12HD12,
12HD13, 12HD15, 12HD15AA,12HD21, 12HD22, 12HD23,
and 12HD23AA: 7 - 9 degrees BTDC
MG Turbo 1985-on: 7 degrees BTDC
MG Metro, 1275 Sport & Vanden Plas engines starting
12HA83HA, 12HB42AA, 12HC14AA, 12GD17, 12HD17AA,
12HD24, 12HD24AA: 10 degrees BTDC
12HC15AA, 12HD25:   5 degrees BTDC

1,275cc engines with unleaded petrol 95 RON specification.
Idle speed 800 rpm
Fast idle speed 1,000 rpm
Valve clearance 0.011 - 0.013 in 0.28 - 0.33 mm)
Ignition timing @ 1,500 rpm, vacuum disconnected:
Engines starting with 12H E41, 12H E42: 13 degrees BTDC
Ignition timing @ 1,500 rpm, vacuum disconnected:
Engines starting with 12H E24, 12H E25, 12H E71, 12H E72,
12H E73, 12H E48:   2 degrees BTDC
Ignition timing @ 1,500 rpm, vacuum disconnected:
Engines starting with 12HF02, 12HF02: 5 degrees BTDC
Valve clearance 0.013 - 0.015 in (0.33 - 0.38 mm)

Cooling system
Thermostat temperature 88 degres C (188 degrees F)
Pressure cap 15 lb/sq in (1.05 kg/sq cm)
Load required to deflect drive belt by 6 to 12 mm
(0.25 to 0.5 in) between water pump and alternator:
22 lb (10 kg)

Steering
Front wheel alignment: Parallel to 0 degrees 25 minutes toe-out
Camber angle: 0 degrees plus or minus 30 minutes
Castor angle: 2 degrees 6 minutes positive plus or minus 2 degrees

Wheels
1.0 litre: 4.5B by 12 in steel
1.3 litre: 5J by 12 in steel (alloy optional)
MG 1300 pre-1984:   5J by 12 in steel (alloy optional)
MG 1300 1984-on: 5J by 12 in alloy
MG Metro Turbo: 5.5J by 13 in alloy

Tyres
Radial ply
Pre-1984
1.0 litre: 135SR 12
MG 1300, Vanden Plas: 155/70R 12
1.3 HLE 1983:   155/70R 12
MG Turbo: 165/60HR 13
1984-1985
1.0 litre & 1.3 Moritz: 150/65 R315
1.0 & 1.3 van: 155/70SR 12
1.3 litre: 160/65 R315
MG 1300:   155/70SR 12
MG Turbo: 165/65HR 13
1986-1990
All models: 160/65 R315
Except
MG Turbo up to 88Y: 165/60HR 13
GTa, Advantage, &
MG Turbo 89MY on   185/55HR 13

Tyre pressures, normal load

	bar	lb.sq in
135SR 12		
front	2.2	32
rear	2.0	28
155/70R 12 & 155/70SR 12		
front	2.0	28
rear, van only	2.2	32
165/60HR 13		
front	2.0	28
rear	2.0	28
150/65 R315		
front	2.1	30
rear	2.0	28
160/65 R315		
front	2.0	28
rear	1.8	26
165/65HR 13 & 165/60HR 13		
front	2.0	28
rear	2.0	28
185/55HR 13		
front	2.0	28
rear	2.0	28

Electrical system

12 volt, negative earth

Alternator pre-1986	Lucas 18 ACR/45 or Motorola 9AR 2683G/45
1986-89	Lucas A127/45 or Lucas A127/55
Fuses	See *Chapter 3, Fuse Factfile*
Starter Motor pre-1986	Lucas M35J Inertia
1986-89	Lucas M79 pre-engaged
Distributor	Lucas or Ducellier with contact breaker points or Lucas electronic with no contact breaker points
Rotation	anticlockwise

Contact breaker gap

Lucas	0.014 in (0.35 mm)
Ducellier	0.015 in (0.38 mm)

Dwell angle (contact breaker ignition only)

Lucas	50 - 59 degrees
Ducellier	55 - 59 degrees

Bulb wattage

Headlamps, Metro & Metro L	45/40
Headlamps, HLE, 1.3S, 1.3HLS	60/50
Sidelamps	4
Direction indictors	21
Reverse lamps	21
Side repeater lamps	5
Stop/tail lamps	5/21
Rear number plate lamp	6
Interior lamp	10
Switch illumination lamps	0.75
Heated rear window switch	1.2
Instrument panel lamps	1.2
Rear fog lamps	21

Capacities (approx)

Engine/gearbox, manual	8.5 pints (4.8 Litres)
Oil filter (manual gearbox)	0.6 pint (0.3 litre)
Engine/gearbox, automatic	8.8 pints (5.0 litres)
Oil filter (auto gearbox)	1 pint (0.6 litre)
Cooling system	8.5 pints (4.8 litres)
Fuel Tank	6.6 gallons (30 litres)

Trim Height

Front	12 7/8 in plus or minus 5/8 in (327 mm plus or minus 15 mm)
Rear (except van & Turbo)	13 1/4 in plus or minus 5/8 in (336 mm plus or minus 15 mm)
Van	13 5/8 in plus or minus 5/8 in (346 mm plus or minus 15 mm)
Turbo	13 in plus or minus 5/8 in (331 plus mm or minus 15 mm)

Brakes

Discs at front, drums at rear, dual hydraulic, servo assistance on 1.3 litre

Disc diameter	8.35 in (213 mm)
Pad thickness	0.37 in (9.6 mm)
Minimum pad thickness	0.125 in (3 mm)
Drum diameter	7 in (177.9 mm)
Minimum lining thickness	0.062 in (1.6 mm)

Chassis lubrication

Suspension	Castrol LM grease

Engine oil

All models: see Page 109

Useful torque wrench settings

	Nm	lb. ft.
Cylinder head	75	55
Rocker cover	5	4
Sparking plugs	25	18
Steering rack mountings	26	19
Road wheels,		
steel	57	42
alloy 1982-84	49	36
alloy 1985-89	57	42
Seat belt mountings	23	17

CHAPTER 9 - TOOLS & EQUIPMENT

Although good tools are not cheap, if you reckon their cost against what you would otherwise spend on professional servicing and repairs, your arithmetic should show you that it doesn't take long to recoup your outlay - and then to start showing a profit!

In fact, there is no need to spend a fortune all at once - most owners who do their own servicing acquire their implements over a long period of time. However, there are some items you simply cannot do without in order to properly carry out the work necessary to keep your car on the road. Therefore, in the following lists, we have concentrated on those items which are likely to be valuable aids to maintaining your car in a good state of tune, and to keep it running sweetly and safely and in addition we have featured some of the tools that are 'nice-to-have' rather than 'must have' because as your tool chest grows, there are some tools that help to make servicing just that bit easier and more thorough to carry out.

Two vital points - firstly always buy the best quality tools you can afford. 'Cheap and cheerful' items may look similar to more expensive implements, but

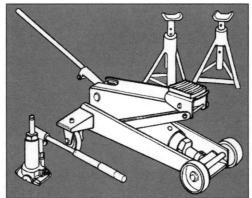

experience shows that they often fail when the going gets tough, and some can even be dangerous. With proper care, good quality tools will last a lifetime, and can be regarded as an investment. The extra outlay is well worth it, in the long run.

Over the years, there have been various nut/bolt/spanner designations. For many years British cars standardised on 'AF', a designation referring to the measurement 'across the flats' of the hexagon nut or bolt head, while the 'foreigners' were 'Metric'. While there are still many 'AF' cars around, all modern cars are 'Metric' of course, apart from American cars. (For the record, 'metric' sizes are also measured across their flats!). Be sure you know which designation applies to your car before you start buying. Your local motor accessory store should be able to advise, or you could all your local main dealer to make sure, if necessary.

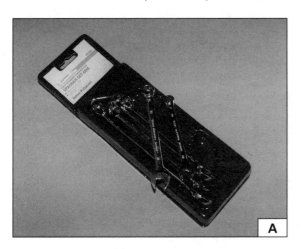

SPANNERS:

A. The two common types of spanner are the ring and the open-ended. The ring spanner grips practically all round the bolt, and is preferable where the bolt is really tight, for an open-ended spanner, merely straddling two flats of the bolt, could slip. On the other hand, the open-end is often quicker and easier to use - so this set of 'Combination' spanners, a ring at one end, open-ended the other, is a nice compromise!

All the tools featured here are available from your local High Street auto-accessory store or Super Store.
Any special tools needed for your car are referred to in Chapter 3.

B. While the 'flatness' of the combination spanners (or of a conventional open-ended spanner) is often useful, there are occasions when only the offset, or 'swan neck' of the conventional ring spanner will do the job - like when having to operate over the top of one bolt in order to undo another.

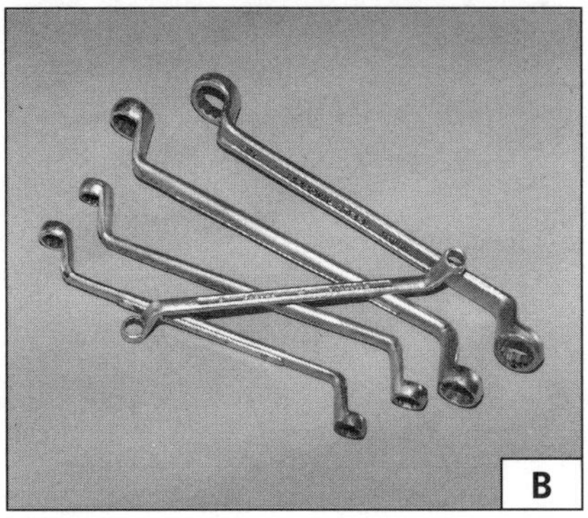
B

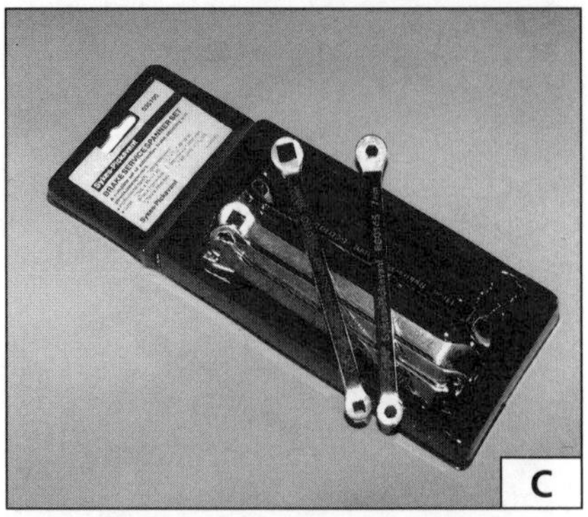
C

Unlike the combination spanners, the conventional ring and open-ended spanners will have a different size at each end. Usually, the AF sizes will rise in sixteenths of an inch, and the metrics by one millimetre - the following sizes will probably cover most of your needs:
AF - 3/8 x 7/16, 1/2 x 9/16, 5/8 x 11/16, 13/16 x 7/8
Metric - 10 x 11, 12 x 13, 14 x 15, 16 x 17

C. The sturdy specialist brake spanner used, for brake adjusters or bleed nipples, is undeniably a wise buy, as mentioned in the brake servicing text. You might not need the set as shown here, but you can choose individual sizes to suit your car, such as 1/4 in. square x 11/32 in. square or 1/4 in. hexagonal x 5/16 in. AF, or perhaps 8 x 10mm hexagonal - there are others.

D. A basic socket set should figure highly on your shopping list, for it will cover your basic spanner sizes and can often solve difficult access or extra-leverage problems. This one is a fairly sophisticated set, and includes a number of useful extras, such as spark plug spanners and Allen key and screwdriver bits. Don't buy more than you need, however, and don't be tempted by cheap, nasty - and often dangerous - market stall socket sets.

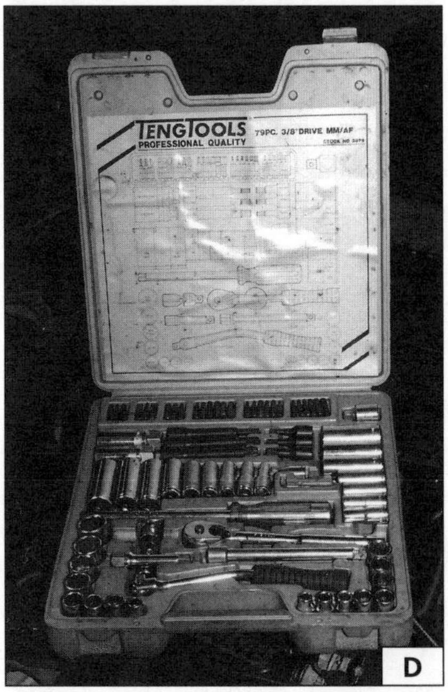

D

E. A torque wrench was also once a luxury, but nowadays it's practically essential, with specific torque settings quoted for many of the nuts and bolts used in modern car engineering. The example shown will cater for most applications, including adjustable wheel-bearing hub nuts, but even the next size up (30-150 lb/ft) in the DIY range will still fall short of the 200-odd lb/ft specified for some hub nuts!

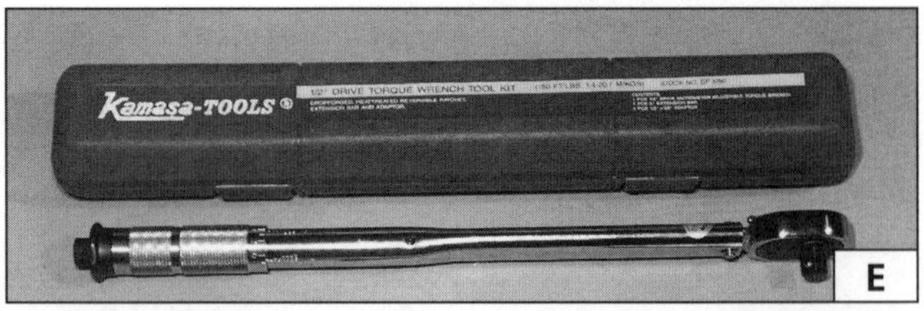

E

F. If you still need a plug spanner, and particularly if your engine features deep-set spark plugs, this Sykes-Pickavant 'extra long plug wrench', combining both 10mm and 14mm sizes, could be a boon. Some plugs are set deeper than the average length of a socket-set spark plug spanner, and if the socket set's extension bar is prone to leaving the spanner socket stuck on the plug, then you could have a problem ...

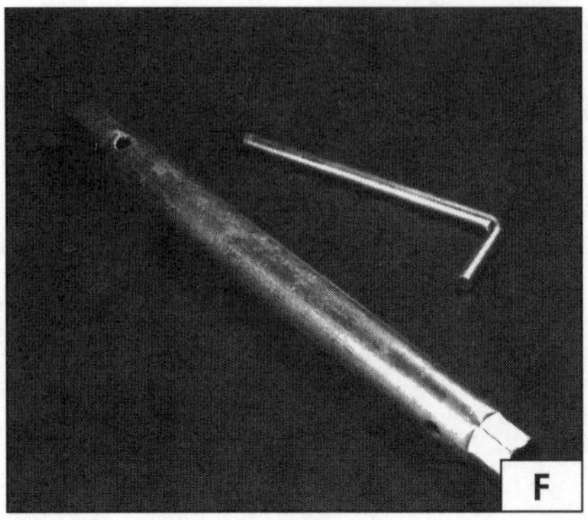
F

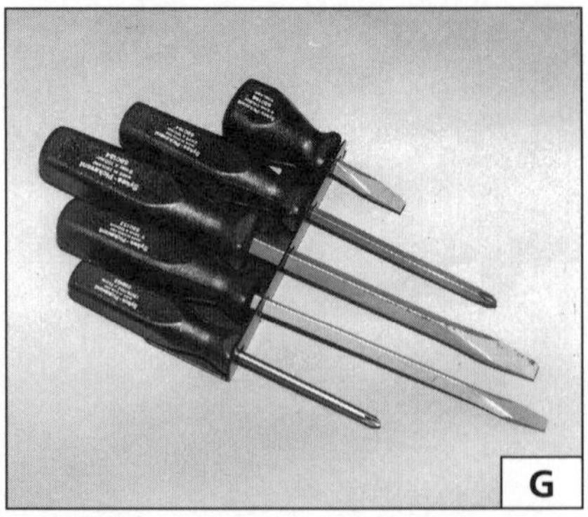
G

SCREWDRIVERS:

G. You will need a selection of screwdrivers, both flat-bladed and cross-headed, long ones, short ones, slim ones, fat ones ...

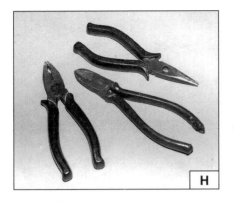

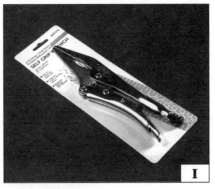

PLIERS:

H. Ordinary combination (or 'engineers') pliers are needed for general work, while a long-nosed pair are handy where access is tight. Their cutting edges are useful for stripping cable insulation, or for snipping wire or trimming split-pin lengths, but you might prefer a pair of specialist side-cutter pliers for such work.

I. Jolly useful as an extra pair of hands, or for gripping such as a rusty nut or bolt really tightly, is a self-grip wrench. This is a long-nose example, but there are also ordinary straight-jaw and round jaw versions.

SUNDRIES:

J. You'll need hammers, including the useful 1lb ball-pein type, plus a hefty copper hammer and maybe a soft (plastic-headed) hammer, too.

K. The wire brush should have brass bristles and as well as an ordinary set of feeler gauges, an 'ignition set' covers most plug and points gap sizes, and includes a points file and a spark plug gap setting tool.

L. You may need a grease gun (although virtually no modern cars have grease points) but you *will* want an oil can, and an oil funnel, and a container of sufficient capacity into which the engine oil can be drained.

M. You may also need a drain plug 'key' suitable for your car unless all the drain plugs are 'bolt'-type hexagons.

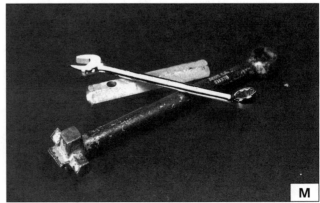

N. Well worthwhile, since some oil filters can be cussedly tight, is some sort of oil filter wrench - this chain-type is a nice example. In extreme cases, even these wrenches can fail to get a grip, in which case, drive an old screwdriver right through the filter and twist it loose.

O. A separate set of hand-held Allen keys is a good idea (they come in metric or Imperial sizes), and an adjustable spanner and a 'Junior' hacksaw will have their uses.

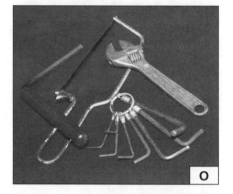

P. For your weekly maintenance checks, you'll need a tyre pressure gauge, tyre tread depth gauge and a footpump - which might, like the example here, have an integral pressure gauge. And whether you're wheel-changing at home or roadside, you will welcome the extremely useful Sykes-Pickavant 'Wheelmaster' wrench, which can be extended to give enough leverage to shift those wheel nuts or bolts that the average car-kit wheelbrace wouldn't even look at - see the wheel-change routine at the start of Chapter 3. Remember to carry the extendable wrench with you in the car!

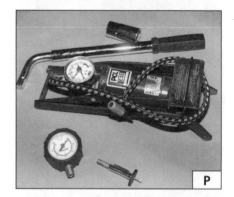

LIFTING:

Q. While the jack supplied with the car *might* be OK for emergency wheel-changes, you would soon tire of trying to use it for servicing operations. Here, you need a good trolley jack, and one of the latest on the market is this 2-ton lifting capacity 'Lift and Lock' example which, as its name suggests, has a built-in fail-safe locking device in the event of hydraulic failure.

R. No matter what sort of jack you use, it is ESSENTIAL that you should not venture beneath a car supported on a jack alone. Having raised it, you need to support it safely and securely. What you need now is definitely NOT house bricks (or any other such potentially dangerous items!) but rather axle stands or wheel-ramps. Adjustable-height stands are essential and both axle stands and ramps should be produced by a 'name' manufacturer, for safety's sake. If you don't need the wheels off, it can be argued that the ramps offer better stability - though you'll benefit from some assistance when it comes to driving upon them. See the start of *Chapter 3*.

TUNING AIDS:

S. As we have said earlier in this chapter and within the servicing sections, the tuning aids that are now available to the DIY market have become practically invaluable 'musts' for the dedicated home mechanic. Any of the Gunson's collection shown here would soon prove their worth. Top of the tree, of course, is their 'Gastester Professional' - don't let its designation suggest that it's not for DIY use, for although it's expensive a group of friends sharing its cost would find their outlay well worth the benefits offered by the unit's Exhaust Gas 'CO' functions, plus its Voltage, Dwell and RPM modes. If it's pure 'multi-meter' you're after, then their 'Digimeter 320' is a tidy little hand-held unit, with clear digital read-outs for such as Volts (DC and household AC) and Amps, Ohms, rpm, and Dwell (degrees and per cent), and its sophistication extends to Frequency, Period and Pulsewidth testing (handy for fuel injection systems), as well as Diode, Resistance and Continuity testing. Also by Gunson's is the powerful 'Timestrobe' xenon timing light, the now not so new, but still novel 'Colortune' and (not shown) the 'Carbalancer'. The latter two devices are virtually invaluable when it comes to car-burettor tuning.

APPENDIX 1 - RECOMMENDED CASTROL LUBRICANTS

ENGINE OIL

1980-1986 models - Non Turbo
Castrol GTX

1987-on models - Non Turbo
Castrol GTX3 Lightec

1982-1986 models - Turbo
Castrol GTX

1987-on models - Turbo
Castrol Formula RS

GEARBOX OIL
Combined with engine.

DIFFERENTIAL
Combined with engine/gearbox.

CV JOINTS
Castrol Moly Grease

BRAKE/CLUTCH FLUID
Castrol Universal Brake and Clutch Fluid

WHEEL BEARINGS
Castrol LM Grease

GREASE POINTS
Castrol LM or Castrol LMX

COOLING SYSTEM
Castrol Antifreeze and Summer Coolant

DOOR LOCKS & HINGES
Castrol Everyman

ELECTRICAL CONNECTIONS
Castrol DWF

NUT & BOLT
Castrol Easing Oil

APPENDIX 2
SPECIALISTS & SUPPLIERS
FEATURED IN THIS BOOK

All of the products and specialists listed below have contributed in various ways to this book. All of the consumer products used are available through regular high street outlets or by mail order from specialist suppliers.

Castrol (UK) Ltd, Burmah House, Pipers Way, Swindon, Wiltshire, SN3 1RE. Tel: 01793 452222
Contact Castrol's Consumer Technical Department Help Line on the above number for assistance with lubrication recommendations.

NGK Spark Plugs (UK) Ltd, 7-8-9 Garrick Industrial Centre, Hendon, London, NW9 6AQ. Tel: 0181 202 2151.
Top quality spark plugs.

Dinol (GB) Limited, Dinol House, 98 Ock Street, Abingdon, Oxford, OX14 5DH. Tel: 01235 530677
Suppliers of Dinitrol rust proofing fluids, and equipped to carry out rustproofing on vehicles.

Gunson Ltd, Coppen Road, Dagenham, Essex, RM8 1NU. Tel: 0181 984 8855.
Electrical and electronic engine tuning equipment.

HPI Autodata, HP Information plc, Dolphin House, P O Box 61, New Street, Salisbury, Wiltshire, SP1 2TB Tel: 01722 422422
Before buying any used car, check it out with HPI Autodata.

Kamasa Tools, Saxon Industries, Lower Everland Road, Hungerford, Berkshire, RG17 0DX. Tel: 01488 684545.
Wide range of hand and power tools, some of which were used in this book.

Rover Group Ltd, International House, Bickenhill Lane, Bickenhill, Birmingham, B37 7HQ. Tel: 0121 782 8000
See your local main dealer in Yellow Pages for Rover parts.

SP Tyres UK Ltd, Fort Dunlop, Birmingham, B24 9QT. Tel: 0121 384 4444.
Manufacturers of Dunlop tyres in both modern and 'period' patterns.

Sykes-Pickavant Group plc, Kilnhouse Lane, Lytham St Annes, Lancs, FY8 3DU. Tel: 01253 721291
Wide range of hand tools and specialist equipment, some of which were used in this book.

APPENDIX 3
SERVICE HISTORY

This Chapter helps you keep track of all the servicing carried out on your vehicle and can even save you money! A vehicle with a Service History is always worth more than one without, and you can make full use of this section, even if you have a garage or mechanic carry out the work for you. It enables you to specify the jobs you want to have carried out to your vehicle and, of course, it enables you to keep that all-important Service History. And even if your vehicle doesn't have a 'history' going back to when it was new, keeping this Chapter complete will add to your vehicle's value when you come to sell it. Mind you, it obviously won't be enough to just to tick the boxes: keep all your receipts when you buy oil, filters and other consumables or parts. That way, you'll also be able to return any faulty parts if needs be.

Buying Parts

Before carrying out a service on your car, you will need to purchase the right parts. Please refer to **Chapter 2, Buying Guide** for information on how to buy the right parts at the right prices and for information on how to find your car's 'identity numbers'; information that you will need in order to buy the right parts, first time!

Month, whichever comes first, is repeated at each one of the following Service Intervals. The same applies to the **6,000 Miles or Six Months** interval: much of it is repeated at **12,000 Miles or Twelve Months.** Every time a Job or set of Jobs is 'repeated' from an earlier Interval, we show it in a tinted area on the page. You can then see more clearly which jobs are unique to the level of Service Interval that you are on.

The Job Lists

Wherever possible, the Jobs listed in this section have been placed in a logical order or placed into groups that will help you make progress on the car. We have tried to save you too much in the way of unnecessary movement by grouping jobs around areas of the car. Therefore, at each Service Interval, you will see the work grouped into Jobs that need carrying out in The Engine Bay, Around The Car or Under The Car.

You'll also see space at each Service Interval for you to write down the date, price and seller's name every time you buy consumables or accessories. And once again, do remember to keep your receipts! There's also space for you to date and sign the Service Record or for a garage's stamp to be applied.

As you move through the Service Intervals. you will notice that the work carried out at say, **1,500 Miles or Every**

You will also find that all the major Intervals, right up to the 'longest', contain Jobs that are unique to that Service Interval. That's why we have continued this Service History right up to the **36,000 Miles or every Three Years** interval. So now, you will be able to service your car and keep a full record of the work, in the knowledge that your car has been looked after as well as anyone could wish for!

Important Note!

The Service Jobs listed here are intended as a check list and a means of keeping a record of your vehicle's service history, **not** as a set of instructions for working on your car. It is most important that you refer to **Chapter 3, Servicing Your Car** for full details of how to carry out each Job listed here and for essential SAFETY information and, see also, **Chapter 1, Safety First!**.

EVERY 500 MILES, WEEKLY, OR BEFORE A LONG JOURNEY

This list is shown, complete, only once. It would have been a bit much to have provided the list 52 times over for use once a week throughout the year! Each job is, however, included with every longer Service list from 3,000 miles/Three Months-on so that each of the 'weekly' Jobs is carried out as part of every service.

Every 500 miles - The Engine Bay

- [ ] Job 1. Engine oil level.
- [ ] Job 2. Clutch fluid level.
- [ ] Job 3. Brake fluid level.
- [ ] Job 4. Battery electrolyte.
- [ ] Job 5. Washer reservoir.
- [ ] Job 6. Cooling system level.
- [ ] Job 7. Heater intake box.
- [ ] Job 8. Horn.

Every 500 miles - Around the Car

- [ ] Job 9. Windscreen washers.
- [ ] Job 10. Windscreen wipers.
- [ ] Job 11. Tyre pressures.
- [ ] Job 12. Check headlights.
- [ ] Job 13. Check front sidelights and direction indicators.
- [ ] Job 14. Side marker indicators.
- [ ] Job 15. Check rear sidelights, indicators and reverse light.
- [ ] Job 16. Check rear fog lights.
- [ ] Job 17. Check rear number plate light.
- [ ] Job 18. Check luggage compartment light. (WHERE FITTED)
- [ ] Job 19. Check interior light.
- [ ] Job 20. Valet bodywork.
- [ ] Job 21. Vacuum interior.

EVERY 1,500 MILES - OR EVERY MONTH, WHICHEVER COMES FIRST

These Jobs are similar to the 500 Mile Jobs but don't need carrying out quite so regularly. Once again, these Jobs are not shown with a separate listing for each 1,500 miles/1 Month interval but they are included as part of every 3,000 miles/Three Months Service list and for every longer Service interval.

Every 1,500 miles - Around the Car

- [ ] Job 22. Check tyre treads.
- [ ] Job 23. Touch-up paintwork.

Every 1,500 miles - Under the Car

- [ ] Job 24. Clean mud traps.

EVERY 3,000 MILES - OR EVERY THREE MONTHS, WHICHEVER COMES FIRST

All the Service Jobs in the tinted area have been carried forward from earlier service intervals and are to be repeated at this service.

Every 3,000 miles - The Engine Bay

First carry out all Jobs listed under earlier Service Intervals as applicable.
- [ ] Job 1. Engine oil level.
- [ ] Job 2. Clutch fluid level.
- [ ] Job 3. Brake fluid level.
- [ ] Job 4. Battery electrolyte.
- [ ] Job 5. Washer reservoir.
- [ ] Job 6. Cooling system level.
- [ ] Job 7. Heater intake box.
- [ ] Job 8. Horn.

- [ ] Job 25. Adjust spark plugs.
- [ ] Job 26. Check HT circuit.
- [ ] Job 27. Check ignition LT circuit.
- [ ] Job 28. Distributor vacuum advance/retard pipe.

- [ ] Job 29. **CONTACT BREAKER IGNITION ONLY** Check cb points.
- [ ] Job 30. **CONTACT BREAKER IGNITION ONLY** Ignition timing dwell.
- [ ] Job 31. **CONTACT BREAKER IGNITION ONLY** Setting ignition dwell.
- [ ] Job 32. Alternator/fan belt.
- [ ] Job 33. Check air filter.
- [ ] Job 34. **OPTIONAL** SU carburettor.
- [ ] Job 35. Pipes and hoses.

Every 3,000 miles - Under the Car

First carry out all Jobs listed under earlier Service Intervals as applicable.
- [ ] Job 24. Clean mud traps.

- [ ] Job 36. Hand brake travel.
- [ ] Job 37. Steering rack gaiters.
- [ ] Job 38. Track rod ends gaiters.
- [ ] Job 39. Drain engine oil.
- [ ] Job 40. Change oil filter.
- [ ] Job 41. Pour in fresh oil.
- [ ] Job 42. Check for oil leaks.
- [ ] Job 43. Check front brake pads.
- [ ] Job 44. Check front discs.
- [ ] Job 45. Check front brake hoses.
- [ ] Job 46. Lubricate front suspension.
- [ ] Job 47. Check steering swivel boots.
- [ ] Job 48. Examine front shock absorber mountings.
- [ ] Job 49. Check front anti-roll bar mountings.
- [ ] Job 50. Examine front suspension unit lower mounting.
- [ ] Job 51. Examine drive shaft gaiters.
- [ ] Job 52. Check front wheelnuts torque.
- [ ] Job 53. Adjust rear brakes.
- [ ] Job 54. Check rear brake pipes.
- [ ] Job 55. Check rear flexible hoses.
- [ ] Job 56. Check rear suspension.
- [ ] Job 57. Lubricate rear suspension.
- [ ] Job 58. Check rear wheelnuts torque.
- [ ] Job 59. Inspect underside.

Every 3,000 miles - Around the Car

First carry out all Jobs listed under earlier Service Intervals as applicable.

- [ ] Job 9. Windscreen washers.
- [ ] Job 10. Windscreen wipers.
- [ ] Job 11. Tyre pressures.
- [ ] Job 12. Check headlights.
- [ ] Job 13. Check front sidelights and direction indicators.
- [ ] Job 14. Side marker indicators.
- [ ] Job 15. Check rear sidelights, indicators and reverse light.
- [ ] Job 16. Check rear fog lights.
- [ ] Job 17. Check rear number plate light.
- [ ] Job 18. Check luggage compartment light. (WHERE FITTED)
- [ ] Job 19. Check interior light.
- [ ] Job 20. Valet bodywork.
- [ ] Job 21. Vacuum interior.
- [ ] Job 22. Check tyre treads.
- [ ] Job 23. Touch-up paintwork.

- [ ] Job 60. Wiper blades and arms.
- [ ] Job 61. Check windscreen.
- [ ] Job 62. Check floors.

Every 3,000 miles - Road Test

First carry out all Jobs listed under earlier Service Intervals as applicable.

- [ ] Job 63. Clean controls.
- [ ] Job 64. Check instruments and controls.
- [ ] Job 65. Throttle and choke cables.
- [ ] Job 66. Road test of brakes and steering.

Date serviced:..

Carried out by: ....
Garage Stamp or signature:

Parts/Accessories purchased (date, parts, source) ....
....
....

EVERY 6,000 MILES - OR EVERY SIX MONTHS, WHICHEVER COMES FIRST

All the Service Jobs in the tinted area have been carried forward from earlier service intervals and are to be repeated at this service.

Every 6,000 miles - The Engine Bay

First carry out all Jobs listed under earlier Service Intervals as applicable.

- [ ] Job 2. Clutch fluid level.
- [ ] Job 3. Brake fluid level.
- [ ] Job 4. Battery electrolyte.
- [ ] Job 5. Washer reservoir.
- [ ] Job 6. Cooling system level.
- [ ] Job 7. Heater intake box.
- [ ] Job 8. Horn.
- [ ] Job 26. Check HT circuit.
- [ ] Job 27. Check ignition LT circuit.
- [ ] Job 28. Distributor vacuum advance/retard pipe.
- [ ] Job 32. Alternator/fan belt.
- [ ] Job 33. Check air filter.
- [ ] Job 35. Pipes and hoses.

- [ ] Job 67. Cooling system.
- [ ] Job 68. Check coolant.
- [ ] Job 69. Check water pump.
- [ ] Job 70. Fit new spark plugs.
- [ ] Job 71. Renew contact breaker points and capacitor.
- [ ] Job 72. Ignition timing.
- [ ] Job 73. Fuel connections.
- [ ] Job 74. Top up carburettor dashpot.
- [ ] Job 75. Overhaul carburettor.
- [ ] Job 76. Setting the carburettor.
- [ ] Job 77. Exhaust emissions.

Every 6,000 miles - Around the Car

First carry out all Jobs listed under earlier Service Intervals as applicable.

- [ ] Job 9. Windscreen washers.
- [ ] Job 10. Windscreen wipers.
- [ ] Job 11. Tyre pressures.
- [ ] Job 12. Check headlights.
- [ ] Job 13. Check front sidelights and direction indicators.
- [ ] Job 14. Side marker indicators.
- [ ] Job 15. Check rear sidelights, indicators and reverse light.
- [ ] Job 16. Check rear fog lights.
- [ ] Job 17. Check rear number plate light.
- [ ] Job 18. Check luggage compartment light. (WHERE FITTED)
- [ ] Job 19. Check interior light.
- [ ] Job 20. Valet bodywork.
- [ ] Job 21. Vacuum interior.
- [ ] Job 22. Check tyre treads.
- [ ] Job 23. Touch-up paintwork.
- [ ] Job 60. Wiper blades and arms.
- [ ] Job 61. Check windscreen.
- [ ] Job 62. Check floors.

- [ ] Job 78. Adjust headlights.
- [ ] Job 79. Front wheel alignment (tracking).
- [ ] Job 80. Front and rear ride heights.
- [ ] Job 81. Fuel filler cap.
- [ ] Job 82. Change alarm remote batteries.
- [ ] Job 83. Bonnet release.
- [ ] Job 84. Bonnet stay.
- [ ] Job 85. Lubricate locks and hinges.
- [ ] Job 86. Check aerial.
- [ ] Job 87. Check seat mountings.
- [ ] Job 88. Check seat belts.

Every 6,000 miles - Under the Car

First carry out all Jobs listed under earlier Service Intervals as applicable.

- [ ] Job 24. Clean mud traps.
- [ ] Job 36. Hand brake travel.
- [ ] Job 37. Steering rack gaiters.
- [ ] Job 38. Track rod ends gaiters.
- [ ] Job 39. Drain engine oil.
- [ ] Job 40. Change oil filter.
- [ ] Job 41. Pour in fresh oil.
- [ ] Job 42. Check for oil leaks.
- [ ] Job 43. Check front brake pads.
- [ ] Job 44. Check front discs.
- [ ] Job 46. Lubricate front suspension.
- [ ] Job 47. Check steering swivel boots.
- [ ] Job 48. Examine front shock absorber mountings.
- [ ] Job 49. Check front anti-roll bar mountings.
- [ ] Job 50. Examine front suspension unit lower mounting.
- [ ] Job 51. Examine drive shaft gaiters.
- [ ] Job 52. Check front wheelnuts torque.
- [ ] Job 53. Adjust rear brakes.
- [ ] Job 55. Check rear flexible hoses.
- [ ] Job 56. Check rear suspension.
- [ ] Job 57. Lubricate rear suspension.
- [ ] Job 58. Check rear wheelnuts torque.
- [ ] Job 59. Inspect underside.

- [ ] Job 89. Front fuel and brake pipes.
- [ ] Job 90. Exhaust system and mountings.
- [ ] Job 91. Front dampers.
- [ ] Job 92. Steering rack mountings.
- [ ] Job 93. Front subframe mountings and engine mountings.
- [ ] Job 94. Rear brake pipes, fuel pipes and Hydragas suspension pipes.
- [ ] Job 95. Rear dampers.
- [ ] Job 96. Rustproofing under the body.
- [ ] Job 97. Clear drain holes.

Every 6,000 miles - Road Test

First carry out all Jobs listed under earlier Service Intervals as applicable.

- [ ] Job 63. Clean controls.
- [ ] Job 64. Check instruments and controls.
- [ ] Job 65. Throttle and choke cables.
- [ ] Job 66. Road test of brakes and steering.

Date serviced:...

Carried out by:...
Garage Stamp or signature:

Parts/Accessories purchased (date, parts, source) ....
....
....
....

EVERY 9,000 MILES - OR EVERY NINE MONTHS, WHICHEVER COMES FIRST

All the Jobs at this Service Interval have been carried forward from earlier Service Intervals and are to be repeated at this service.

Every 9,000 miles - The Engine Bay

- [ ] Job 1. Engine oil level.
- [ ] Job 2. Clutch fluid level.
- [ ] Job 3. Brake fluid level.
- [ ] Job 4. Battery electrolyte.
- [ ] Job 5. Washer reservoir.
- [ ] Job 6. Cooling system level.
- [ ] Job 7. Heater intake box.
- [ ] Job 8. Horn.
- [ ] Job 26. Check HT circuit.
- [ ] Job 27. Check ignition LT circuit.
- [ ] Job 28. Distributor, vacuum advance/retard pipe.
- [ ] Job 32. Alternator/fan belt.
- [ ] Job 33. Check air filter.
- [ ] Job 34. **OPTIONAL** SU carburettor.
- [ ] Job 35. Pipes and hoses.

Every 9,000 miles - Around The Car

- Job 9. Windscreen washers.
- Job 10. Windscreen wipers.
- Job 11. Tyre pressures.
- Job 12. Check headlights.
- Job 13. Check front sidelights and direction indicators.
- Job 14. Side marker indicators.
- Job 15. Check rear sidelights, indicators and reverse light.
- Job 16. Check rear fog lights.
- Job 17. Check rear number plate light.
- Job 18. Check luggage compartment light. (WHERE FITTED)
- Job 19. Check interior light.
- Job 20. Valet bodywork.
- Job 21. Vacuum interior.
- Job 22. Check tyre treads.
- Job 23. Touch-up paintwork.
- Job 60. Wiper blades and arms.
- Job 61. Check windscreen.
- Job 62. Check floors.

Every 9,000 miles - Under the Car

- Job 24. Clean mud traps.
- Job 36. Hand brake travel.
- Job 37. Steering rack gaiters.
- Job 38. Track rod ends gaiters.
- Job 39. Drain engine oil.
- Job 40. Change oil filter.
- Job 41. Pour in fresh oil.
- Job 42. Check for oil leaks.
- Job 43. Check front brake pads.
- Job 44. Check front discs.
- Job 46. Lubricate front suspension.
- Job 47. Check steering swivel boots.
- Job 48. Examine front shock absorber mountings.
- Job 49. Check front anti-roll bar mountings.
- Job 50. Examine front suspension unit lower mounting.

- Job 51. Examine drive shaft gaiters.
- Job 52. Check front wheelnuts torque.
- Job 53. Adjust rear brakes.
- Job 55. Check rear flexible hoses.
- Job 56. Check rear suspension.
- Job 57. Lubricate rear suspension.
- Job 58. Check rear wheelnuts torque.
- Job 59. Inspect underside.

Every 9,000 miles - Road Test

First carry out all Jobs listed under earlier Service Intervals as applicable.

- Job 63. Clean controls.
- Job 64. Check instruments and controls.
- Job 65. Throttle and choke cables.
- Job 66. Road test of brakes and steering.

Date serviced:...

Carried out by:..
Garage Stamp or signature:

Parts/Accessories purchased (date, parts, source) ....
....
....
....

EVERY 12,000 MILES - OR EVERY TWELVE MONTHS - WHICHEVER COMES FIRST

All the Service Jobs in the tinted area have been carried forward from earlier service intervals and are to be repeated at this service.

Every 12,000 miles - The Engine Bay

First carry out all Jobs listed under earlier Service Intervals as applicable.

- Job 2. Clutch fluid level.
- Job 3. Brake fluid level.
- Job 4. Battery electrolyte.
- Job 5. Washer reservoir.
- Job 6. Cooling system level.
- Job 7. Heater intake box.
- Job 8. Horn.
- Job 26. Check HT circuit.
- Job 27. Check ignition LT circuit.
- Job 28. Distributor vacuum advance/retard pipe.
- Job 32. Alternator/fan belt.
- Job 33. Check air filter.
- Job 35. Pipes and hoses.
- Job 68. Check coolant.
- Job 69. Check water pump.
- Job 70. Fit new spark plugs.
- Job 71. Renew contact breaker points and capacitor.
- Job 72. Ignition timing.
- Job 73. Fuel connections.
- Job 74. Top up carburettor dashpot.
- Job 75. Overhaul carburettor.
- Job 76. Setting the carburettor.
- Job 77. Exhaust emissions.

- Job 98. Breather hoses.
- Job 99. Oil filler cap.
- Job 100. Oil leaks.
- Job 101. Clean radiator.
- Job 102. Check valve clearances.
- Job 103. Clutch stop clearances and mechanism.
- Job 104. Cylinder compressions.

SERVICE HISTORY

Every 12,000 miles - Around the Car

First carry out all Jobs listed under earlier Service Intervals as applicable.

- [ ] Job 9. Windscreen washers.
- [ ] Job 10. Windscreen wipers.
- [ ] Job 11. Tyre pressures.
- [ ] Job 12. Check headlights.
- [ ] Job 13. Check front sidelights and direction indicators.
- [ ] Job 14. Side marker indicators.
- [ ] Job 15. Check rear sidelights, indicators and reverse light.
- [ ] Job 16. Check rear fog lights.
- [ ] Job 17. Check rear number plate light.
- [ ] Job 18. Check luggage compartment light. (WHERE FITTED)
- [ ] Job 19. Check interior light.
- [ ] Job 20. Valet bodywork.
- [ ] Job 21. Vacuum interior.
- [ ] Job 22. Check tyre treads.
- [ ] Job 23. Touch-up paintwork.
- [ ] Job 60. Wiper blades and arms.
- [ ] Job 61. Check windscreen.
- [ ] Job 62. Check floors.
- [ ] Job 78. Adjust headlights.
- [ ] Job 79. Front wheel alignment (tracking).
- [ ] Job 80. Front and rear ride heights.
- [ ] Job 81. Fuel filler cap.
- [ ] Job 82. Change alarm remote batteries.
- [ ] Job 83. Bonnet release.
- [ ] Job 84. Bonnet stay.
- [ ] Job 85. Lubricate locks and hinges.
- [ ] Job 86. Check aerial.
- [ ] Job 87. Check seat mountings.
- [ ] Job 88. Check seat belts.

- [ ] Job 105. Test shock absorbers.
- [ ] Job 106. Toolkit and jack.

Every 12,000 miles - Under the Car

First carry out all Jobs listed under earlier Service Intervals as applicable.

- [ ] Job 24. Clean mud traps.
- [ ] Job 36. Hand brake travel.
- [ ] Job 37. Steering rack gaiters.
- [ ] Job 38. Track rod ends gaiters.
- [ ] Job 39. Drain engine oil.
- [ ] Job 40. Change oil filter.
- [ ] Job 41. Pour in fresh oil.
- [ ] Job 42. Check for oil leaks.
- [ ] Job 43. Check front brake pads.
- [ ] Job 44. Check front discs.
- [ ] Job 46. Lubricate front suspension.
- [ ] Job 47. Check steering swivel boots.
- [ ] Job 48. Examine front shock absorber mountings.
- [ ] Job 49. Check front anti-roll bar mountings.
- [ ] Job 50. Examine front suspension unit lower mounting.
- [ ] Job 51. Examine drive shaft gaiters.
- [ ] Job 52. Check front wheelnuts torque.
- [ ] Job 55. Check rear flexible hoses.
- [ ] Job 56. Check rear suspension.
- [ ] Job 57. Lubricate rear suspension.
- [ ] Job 58. Check rear wheelnuts torque.
- [ ] Job 59. Inspect underside.
- [ ] Job 89. Front fuel and brake pipes.
- [ ] Job 90. Exhaust system and mountings.
- [ ] Job 91. Front dampers.
- [ ] Job 92. Steering rack mountings.
- [ ] Job 93. Front subframe mountings and engine mountings.
- [ ] Job 94. Rear brake pipes, fuel pipes and Hydragas suspension pipes.
- [ ] Job 95. Rear dampers.
- [ ] Job 96. Rustproofing under the body.
- [ ] Job 97. Clear drain holes.

- [ ] Job 107. Front suspension bushes.
- [ ] Job 108. Check steering swivels.
- [ ] Job 109. Check steering ball joints and rack.
- [ ] Job 110. Check steering wheel free play.

- [ ] Job 111. Front callipers.
- [ ] Job 112. Rear brake inspection and overhaul.
- [ ] Job 113. Renew rear brake shoes.
- [ ] Job 114. Top-up rustproofing.

Every 12,000 miles - Road Test

First carry out all Jobs listed under earlier Service Intervals as applicable.

- [ ] Job 63. Clean controls.
- [ ] Job 64. Check instruments and controls.
- [ ] Job 65. Throttle and choke cables.
- [ ] Job 66. Road test of brakes and steering.

Date serviced:..

Carried out by:..
Garage Stamp or signature:

Parts/Accessories purchased (date, parts, source)..
....
....
....

EVERY 15,000 MILES - OR EVERY FIFTEEN MONTHS, WHICHEVER COMES FIRST

All the Jobs at this Service Interval have been carried forward from earlier Service Intervals and are to be repeated at this service.

Every 15,000 miles - The Engine Bay

- [ ] Job 1. Engine oil level.
- [ ] Job 2. Clutch fluid level.
- [ ] Job 3. Brake fluid level.
- [ ] Job 4. Battery electrolyte.
- [ ] Job 5. Washer reservoir.
- [ ] Job 6. Cooling system level.
- [ ] Job 7. Heater intake box.
- [ ] Job 8. Horn.
- [ ] Job 26. Check HT circuit.
- [ ] Job 27. Check ignition LT circuit.
- [ ] Job 28. Distributor vacuum advance/retard pipe.
- [ ] Job 32. Alternator/fan belt.
- [ ] Job 33. Check air filter.
- [ ] Job 34. **OPTIONAL** SU carburettor.
- [ ] Job 35. Pipes and hoses.

Every 15,000 miles - Around The Car

- [ ] Job 9. Windscreen washers.
- [ ] Job 10. Windscreen wipers.
- [ ] Job 11. Tyre pressures.
- [ ] Job 12. Check headlights.
- [ ] Job 13. Check front sidelights and direction indicators.
- [ ] Job 14. Side marker indicators.
- [ ] Job 15. Check rear sidelights, indicators and reverse light.
- [ ] Job 16. Check rear fog lights.
- [ ] Job 17. Check rear number plate light.
- [ ] Job 18. Check luggage compartment light. (WHERE FITTED)
- [ ] Job 19. Check interior light.
- [ ] Job 20. Valet bodywork.
- [ ] Job 21. Vacuum interior.
- [ ] Job 22. Check tyre treads.
- [ ] Job 23. Touch-up paintwork.
- [ ] Job 60. Wiper blades and arms.
- [ ] Job 61. Check windscreen.
- [ ] Job 62. Check floors.

Every 15,000 miles - Under the Car

- [ ] Job 24. Clean mud traps.
- [ ] Job 36. Hand brake travel.
- [ ] Job 37. Steering rack gaiters.
- [ ] Job 38. Track rod ends gaiters.
- [ ] Job 39. Drain engine oil.
- [ ] Job 40. Change oil filter.
- [ ] Job 41. Pour in fresh oil.
- [ ] Job 42. Check for oil leaks.
- [ ] Job 43. Check front brake pads.
- [ ] Job 44. Check front discs.
- [ ] Job 46. Lubricate front suspension.
- [ ] Job 47. Check steering swivel boots.
- [ ] Job 48. Examine front shock absorber mountings.
- [ ] Job 49. Check front anti-roll bar mountings.
- [ ] Job 50. Examine front suspension unit lower mounting.

- [ ] Job 51. Examine drive shaft gaiters.
- [ ] Job 52. Check front wheelnuts torque.
- [ ] Job 53. Adjust rear brakes.
- [ ] Job 55. Check rear flexible hoses.
- [ ] Job 56. Check rear suspension.
- [ ] Job 57. Lubricate rear suspension.
- [ ] Job 58. Check rear wheelnuts torque.
- [ ] Job 59. Inspect underside.

Every 15,000 miles - Road Test

First carry out all Jobs listed under earlier Service Intervals as applicable.

- [ ] Job 63. Clean controls.
- [ ] Job 64. Check instruments and controls.
- [ ] Job 65. Throttle and choke cables.
- [ ] Job 66. Road test of brakes and steering.

Date serviced:...

Carried out by: ....
Garage Stamp or signature:

Parts/Accessories purchased (date, parts, source) ....
....
....
....

EVERY 18,000 MILES - OR EVERY EIGHTEEN MONTHS, WHICHEVER COMES FIRST

All the Jobs at this Service Interval have been carried forward from earlier Service Intervals and are to be repeated at this service.

Every 18,000 miles - The Engine Bay

First carry out all Jobs listed under earlier Service Intervals as applicable.

- [ ] Job 2. Clutch fluid level.
- [ ] Job 3. Brake fluid level.
- [ ] Job 4. Battery electrolyte.
- [ ] Job 5. Washer reservoir.
- [ ] Job 6. Cooling system level.
- [ ] Job 7. Heater intake box.
- [ ] Job 8. Horn.
- [ ] Job 26. Check HT circuit.
- [ ] Job 27. Check ignition LT circuit.
- [ ] Job 28. Distributor vacuum advance/retard pipe.
- [ ] Job 32. Alternator/fan belt.
- [ ] Job 33. Check air filter.
- [ ] Job 35. Pipes and hoses.
- [ ] Job 68. Check coolant.
- [ ] Job 69. Check water pump.
- [ ] Job 70. Fit new spark plugs.
- [ ] Job 71. Renew contact breaker points and capacitor.
- [ ] Job 72. Ignition timing.
- [ ] Job 73. Fuel connections.
- [ ] Job 74. Top up carburettor dashpot.
- [ ] Job 75. Overhaul carburettor.
- [ ] Job 76. Setting the carburettor.
- [ ] Job 77. Exhaust emissions.

Every 18,000 miles - Around the Car

First carry out all Jobs listed under earlier Service Intervals as applicable.

- [ ] Job 9. Windscreen washers.
- [ ] Job 10. Windscreen wipers.
- [ ] Job 11. Tyre pressures.
- [ ] Job 12. Check headlights.
- [ ] Job 13. Check front sidelights and direction indicators.
- [ ] Job 14. Side marker indicators.
- [ ] Job 15. Check rear sidelights, indicators and reverse light.
- [ ] Job 16. Check rear fog lights.
- [ ] Job 17. Check rear number plate light.
- [ ] Job 18. Check luggage compartment light. (WHERE FITTED)
- [ ] Job 19. Check interior light.
- [ ] Job 20. Valet bodywork.
- [ ] Job 21. Vacuum interior.
- [ ] Job 22. Check tyre treads.
- [ ] Job 23. Touch-up paintwork.
- [ ] Job 60. Wiper blades and arms.
- [ ] Job 61. Check windscreen.
- [ ] Job 62. Check floors.
- [ ] Job 78. Adjust headlights.
- [ ] Job 79. Front wheel alignment (tracking).
- [ ] Job 80. Front and rear ride heights.
- [ ] Job 81. Fuel filler cap.
- [ ] Job 82. Change alarm remote batteries.
- [ ] Job 83. Bonnet release.
- [ ] Job 84. Bonnet stay.
- [ ] Job 85. Lubricate locks and hinges.
- [ ] Job 86. Check aerial.
- [ ] Job 87. Check seat mountings.
- [ ] Job 88. Check seat belts.

Every 18,000 miles - Under the Car

First carry out all Jobs listed under earlier Service Intervals as applicable.

- [ ] Job 24. Clean mud traps.
- [ ] Job 36. Hand brake travel.
- [ ] Job 37. Steering rack gaiters.
- [ ] Job 38. Track rod ends gaiters.
- [ ] Job 39. Drain engine oil.
- [ ] Job 40. Change oil filter.
- [ ] Job 41. Pour in fresh oil.
- [ ] Job 42. Check for oil leaks.
- [ ] Job 43. Check front brake pads.
- [ ] Job 44. Check front discs.
- [ ] Job 46. Lubricate front suspension.
- [ ] Job 47. Check steering swivel boots.
- [ ] Job 48. Examine front shock absorber mountings.
- [ ] Job 49. Check front anti-roll bar mountings.
- [ ] Job 50. Examine front suspension unit lower mounting.
- [ ] Job 51. Examine drive shaft gaiters.
- [ ] Job 52. Check front wheelnuts torque.
- [ ] Job 55. Check rear flexible hoses.
- [ ] Job 56. Check rear suspension.
- [ ] Job 57. Lubricate rear suspension.
- [ ] Job 58. Check rear wheelnuts torque.
- [ ] Job 59. Inspect underside.
- [ ] Job 89. Front fuel and brake pipes.
- [ ] Job 90. Exhaust system and mountings.
- [ ] Job 91. Front dampers.
- [ ] Job 92. Steering rack mountings.
- [ ] Job 93. Front subframe mountings and engine mountings.
- [ ] Job 94. Rear brake pipes, fuel pipes and Hydragas suspension pipes.
- [ ] Job 95. Rear dampers.
- [ ] Job 96. Rustproofing under the body.
- [ ] Job 97. Clear drain holes.

Every 18,000 miles - Road Test

First carry out all Jobs listed under earlier Service Intervals as applicable.

- [ ] Job 63. Clean controls.
- [ ] Job 64. Check instruments and controls.
- [ ] Job 65. Throttle and choke cables.
- [ ] Job 66. Road test of brakes and steering.

EVERY 21,000 MILES - OR EVERY TWENTY ONE MONTHS, WHICHEVER COMES FIRST

All the Jobs at this Service Interval have been carried forward from earlier Service Intervals and are to be repeated at this service.

Every 21,000 miles - The Engine Bay

- [ ] Job 1. Engine oil level.
- [ ] Job 2. Clutch fluid level.
- [ ] Job 3. Brake fluid level.
- [ ] Job 4. Battery electrolyte.
- [ ] Job 5. Washer reservoir.
- [ ] Job 6. Cooling system level.
- [ ] Job 7. Heater intake box.
- [ ] Job 8. Horn.
- [ ] Job 26. Check HT circuit.
- [ ] Job 27. Check ignition LT circuit.
- [ ] Job 28. Distributor vacuum advance/retard pipe.
- [ ] Job 32. Alternator/fan belt.
- [ ] Job 33. Check air filter.
- [ ] Job 34. OPTIONAL SU carburettor.
- [ ] Job 35. Pipes and hoses.

Date serviced:...

Carried out by: ....
Garage Stamp or signature:

Parts/Accessories purchased (date, parts, source) ....
....
....
....

Every 21,000 miles - Around the Car

- [ ] Job 9. Windscreen washers.
- [ ] Job 10. Windscreen wipers.
- [ ] Job 11. Tyre pressures.
- [ ] Job 12. Check headlights.
- [ ] Job 13. Check front sidelights and direction indicators.
- [ ] Job 14. Side marker indicators.
- [ ] Job 15. Check rear sidelights, indicators and reverse light.
- [ ] Job 16. Check rear fog lights.
- [ ] Job 17. Check rear number plate light.
- [ ] Job 18. Check luggage compartment light. (WHERE FITTED)
- [ ] Job 19. Check interior light.
- [ ] Job 20. Valet bodywork.
- [ ] Job 21. Vacuum interior.
- [ ] Job 22. Check tyre treads.
- [ ] Job 23. Touch-up paintwork.
- [ ] Job 60. Wiper blades and arms.
- [ ] Job 61. Check windscreen.
- [ ] Job 62. Check floors.

Every 21,000 miles - Under the Car

- [ ] Job 24. Clean mud traps.
- [ ] Job 36. Hand brake travel.
- [ ] Job 37. Steering rack gaiters.
- [ ] Job 38. Track rod ends gaiters.
- [ ] Job 39. Drain engine oil.
- [ ] Job 40. Change oil filter.
- [ ] Job 41. Pour in fresh oil.
- [ ] Job 42. Check for oil leaks.
- [ ] Job 43. Check front brake pads.
- [ ] Job 44. Check front discs.
- [ ] Job 46. Lubricate front suspension.
- [ ] Job 47. Check steering swivel boots.
- [ ] Job 48. Examine front shock absorber mountings.
- [ ] Job 49. Check front anti-roll bar mountings.
- [ ] Job 50. Examine front suspension unit lower mounting.

- [ ] Job 51. Examine drive shaft gaiters.
- [ ] Job 52. Check front wheelnuts torque.
- [ ] Job 53. Adjust rear brakes.
- [ ] Job 55. Check rear flexible hoses.
- [ ] Job 56. Check rear suspension.
- [ ] Job 57. Lubricate rear suspension.
- [ ] Job 58. Check rear wheelnuts torque.
- [ ] Job 59. Inspect underside.

Every 21,000 miles - Road Test

First carry out all Jobs listed under earlier Service Intervals as applicable.

- [ ] Job 63. Clean controls.
- [ ] Job 64. Check instruments and controls.
- [ ] Job 65. Throttle and choke cables.
- [ ] Job 66. Road test of brakes and steering.

Date serviced:..

Carried out by: ....
Garage Stamp or signature:

Parts/Accessories purchased (date, parts, source) ....

....

....

....

EVERY 24,000 MILES - OR EVERY TWENTY FOUR MONTHS, WHICHEVER COMES FIRST

All the Service Jobs in the tinted area have been carried forward from earlier service intervals and are to be repeated at this service.

Every 24,000 miles - The Engine Bay

First carry out all Jobs listed under earlier Service Intervals as applicable.

- [ ] Job 2. Clutch fluid level.
- [ ] Job 4. Battery electrolyte.
- [ ] Job 5. Washer reservoir.
- [ ] Job 7. Heater intake box.
- [ ] Job 8. Horn.
- [ ] Job 26. Check HT circuit.
- [ ] Job 27. Check ignition LT circuit.
- [ ] Job 28. Distributor vacuum advance/retard pipe.
- [ ] Job 33. Check air filter.
- [ ] Job 35. Pipes and hoses.
- [ ] Job 67. Cooling system.
- [ ] Job 68. Check coolant.
- [ ] Job 69. Check water pump.
- [ ] Job 70. Fit new spark plugs.
- [ ] Job 71. Renew contact breaker points and capacitor.
- [ ] Job 72. Ignition timing.
- [ ] Job 73. Fuel connections.
- [ ] Job 74. Top up carburettor dashpot.
- [ ] Job 75. Overhaul carburettor.
- [ ] Job 76. Setting the carburettor.
- [ ] Job 77. Exhaust emissions.
- [ ] Job 98. Breather hoses.
- [ ] Job 99. Oil filler cap.
- [ ] Job 100. Oil leaks.
- [ ] Job 101. Clean radiator.
- [ ] Job 102. Check valve clearances.
- [ ] Job 103. Clutch stop clearances and mechanism.
- [ ] Job 104. Cylinder compressions.

- [ ] Job 115. Change fuel filter.
- [ ] Job 116. Drain and refill cooling system.
- [ ] Job 117. Renew radiator pressure cap.
- [ ] Job 118. Renew fan belt.
- [ ] Job 119. Change brake servo filter.
- [ ] Job 120. Check air intake flap.

Every 24,000 miles - Under the Car

First carry out all Jobs listed under earlier Service Intervals as applicable.

- [ ] Job 24. Clean mud traps.
- [ ] Job 36. Hand brake travel.
- [ ] Job 37. Steering rack gaiters.
- [ ] Job 38. Track rod ends gaiters.
- [ ] Job 39. Drain engine oil.
- [ ] Job 40. Change oil filter.
- [ ] Job 41. Pour in fresh oil.
- [ ] Job 42. Check for oil leaks.
- [ ] Job 43. Check front brake pads.
- [ ] Job 44. Check front discs.
- [ ] Job 46. Lubricate front suspension.
- [ ] Job 47. Check steering swivel boots.
- [ ] Job 48. Examine front shock absorber mountings.
- [ ] Job 49. Check front anti-roll bar mountings.
- [ ] Job 50. Examine front suspension unit lower mounting.
- [ ] Job 51. Examine drive shaft gaiters.
- [ ] Job 52. Check front wheelnuts torque.
- [ ] Job 55. Check rear flexible hoses.
- [ ] Job 56. Check rear suspension.
- [ ] Job 57. Lubricate rear suspension.
- [ ] Job 58. Check rear wheelnuts torque.
- [ ] Job 59. Inspect underside.
- [ ] Job 89. Front fuel and brake pipes.
- [ ] Job 90. Exhaust system and mountings.
- [ ] Job 91. Front dampers.
- [ ] Job 92. Steering rack mountings.
- [ ] Job 93. Front subframe mountings and engine mountings.
- [ ] Job 94. Rear brake pipes, fuel pipes and Hydragas suspension pipes.
- [ ] Job 95. Rear dampers.

☐ Job 96. Rustproofing under the body.

☐ Job 97. Clear drain holes.

☐ Job 107. Front suspension bushes.

☐ Job 108. Check steering swivels.

☐ Job 109. Check steering ball joints and rack.

☐ Job 110. Check steering wheel free play.

☐ Job 111. Front callipers.

☐ Job 112. Rear brake inspection and overhaul.

☐ Job 113. Renew rear brake shoes.

☐ Job 114. Top-up rustproofing.

☐ Job 121. Flushing oil.

☐ Job 122. Suspension mountings.

☐ Job 123. Brake discs.

☐ Job 124. Renew brake fluid.

Every 24,000 miles - Around the Car

First carry out all Jobs listed under earlier Service Intervals as applicable.

☐ Job 9. Windscreen washers.

☐ Job 10. Windscreen wipers.

☐ Job 11. Tyre pressures.

☐ Job 12. Check headlights.

☐ Job 13. Check front sidelights and direction indicators.

☐ Job 14. Side marker indicators.

☐ Job 15. Check rear sidelights, indicators and reverse light.

☐ Job 16. Check rear fog lights.

☐ Job 17. Check rear number plate light.

☐ Job 18. Check luggage compartment light. (WHERE FITTED)

☐ Job 19. Check interior light.

☐ Job 20. Valet bodywork.

☐ Job 21. Vacuum interior.

☐ Job 22. Check tyre treads.

☐ Job 23. Touch-up paintwork.

☐ Job 60. Wiper blades and arms.

☐ Job 61. Check windscreen.

☐ Job 62. Check floors.

☐ Job 78. Adjust headlights.

☐ Job 79. Front wheel alignment (tracking).

☐ Job 80. Front and rear ride heights.

☐ Job 81. Fuel filler cap.

☐ Job 82. Change alarm remote batteries.

☐ Job 83. Bonnet release.

☐ Job 84. Bonnet stay.

☐ Job 85. Lubricate locks and hinges.

☐ Job 86. Check aerial.

☐ Job 87. Check seat mountings.

☐ Job 88. Check seat belts.

☐ Job 105. Test shock absorbers.

☐ Job 106. Toolkit and jack.

☐ Job 125. Window regulators.

☐ Job 126. Door gear.

☐ Job 127. Light seals.

Every 24,000 miles - Road Test

First carry out all Jobs listed under earlier Service Intervals as applicable.

☐ Job 63. Clean controls.

☐ Job 64. Check instruments and controls.

☐ Job 65. Throttle and choke cables.

☐ Job 66. Road test of brakes and steering.

EVERY 27,000 MILES - OR EVERY TWENTY SEVEN MONTHS, WHICHEVER COMES FIRST

All the Jobs at this Service Interval have been carried forward from earlier Service Intervals and are to be repeated at this service.

Every 27,000 miles - The Engine Bay

☐ Job 1. Engine oil level.

☐ Job 2. Clutch fluid level.

☐ Job 3. Brake fluid level.

☐ Job 4. Battery electrolyte.

☐ Job 5. Washer reservoir.

☐ Job 6. Cooling system level.

☐ Job 7. Heater intake box.

☐ Job 8. Horn.

☐ Job 26. Check HT circuit.

☐ Job 27. Check ignition LT circuit.

☐ Job 28. Distributor vacuum advance/retard pipe.

☐ Job 32. Alternator/fan belt.

☐ Job 33. Check air filter.

☐ Job 34. **OPTIONAL** SU carburettor.

☐ Job 35. Pipes and hoses.

Date serviced:...

Carried out by: ....
Garage Stamp or signature:

Parts/Accessories purchased (date, parts,

source) ....

....

....

....

SERVICE HISTORY

Every 27,000 miles - Around the Car

- ☐ Job 9. Windscreen washers.
- ☐ Job 10. Windscreen wipers.
- ☐ Job 11. Tyre pressures.
- ☐ Job 12. Check headlights.
- ☐ Job 13. Check front sidelights and direction indicators.
- ☐ Job 14. Side marker indicators.
- ☐ Job 15. Check rear sidelights, indicators and reverse light.
- ☐ Job 16. Check rear fog lights.
- ☐ Job 17. Check rear number plate light.
- ☐ Job 18. Check luggage compartment light. (WHERE FITTED)
- ☐ Job 19. Check interior light.
- ☐ Job 20. Valet bodywork.
- ☐ Job 21. Vacuum interior.
- ☐ Job 22. Check tyre treads.
- ☐ Job 23. Touch-up paintwork.
- ☐ Job 60. Wiper blades and arms.
- ☐ Job 61. Check windscreen.
- ☐ Job 62. Check floors.

Every 27,000 miles - Under the Car

- ☐ Job 24. Clean mud traps.
- ☐ Job 36. Hand brake travel.
- ☐ Job 37. Steering rack gaiters.
- ☐ Job 38. Track rod ends gaiters.
- ☐ Job 39. Drain engine oil.
- ☐ Job 40. Change oil filter.
- ☐ Job 41. Pour in fresh oil.
- ☐ Job 42. Check for oil leaks.
- ☐ Job 43. Check front brake pads.
- ☐ Job 44. Check front discs.
- ☐ Job 46. Lubricate front suspension.
- ☐ Job 47. Check steering swivel boots.
- ☐ Job 48. Examine front shock absorber mountings.
- ☐ Job 49. Check front anti-roll bar mountings.
- ☐ Job 50. Examine front suspension unit lower mounting.

- ☐ Job 51. Examine drive shaft gaiters.
- ☐ Job 52. Check front wheelnuts torque.
- ☐ Job 53. Adjust rear brakes.
- ☐ Job 55. Check rear flexible hoses.
- ☐ Job 56. Check rear suspension.
- ☐ Job 57. Lubricate rear suspension.
- ☐ Job 58. Check rear wheelnuts torque.
- ☐ Job 59. Inspect underside.

Every 27,000 miles - Road Test

First carry out all Jobs listed under earlier Service Intervals as applicable.

- ☐ Job 63. Clean controls.
- ☐ Job 64. Check instruments and controls.
- ☐ Job 65. Throttle and choke cables.
- ☐ Job 66. Road test of brakes and steering.

Date serviced:...

Carried out by: ....
Garage Stamp or signature:

Parts/Accessories purchased (date, parts, source) ....
....
....
....

EVERY 30,000 MILES - OR EVERY THIRTY MONTHS, WHICHEVER COMES FIRST

All the Jobs at this Service Interval have been carried forward from earlier Service Intervals and are to be repeated at this service.

Every 30,000 miles - The Engine Bay

First carry out all Jobs listed under earlier Service Intervals as applicable.

- ☐ Job 2. Clutch fluid level.
- ☐ Job 3. Brake fluid level.
- ☐ Job 4. Battery electrolyte.
- ☐ Job 5. Washer reservoir.
- ☐ Job 6. Cooling system level.
- ☐ Job 7. Heater intake box.
- ☐ Job 8. Horn.
- ☐ Job 26. Check HT circuit.
- ☐ Job 27. Check ignition LT circuit.
- ☐ Job 28. Distributor vacuum advance/retard pipe.
- ☐ Job 32. Alternator/fan belt.
- ☐ Job 33. Check air filter.
- ☐ Job 35. Pipes and hoses.
- ☐ Job 68. Check coolant.
- ☐ Job 69. Check water pump.
- ☐ Job 70. Fit new spark plugs.
- ☐ Job 71. Renew contact breaker points and capacitor.
- ☐ Job 72. Ignition timing.
- ☐ Job 73. Fuel connections.
- ☐ Job 74. Top up carburettor dashpot.
- ☐ Job 75. Overhaul carburettor.
- ☐ Job 76. Setting the carburettor.
- ☐ Job 77. Exhaust emissions.

Every 30,000 miles - Around the Car

First carry out all Jobs listed under earlier Service Intervals as applicable.

- [ ] Job 9. Windscreen washers.
- [ ] Job 10. Windscreen wipers.
- [ ] Job 11. Tyre pressures.
- [ ] Job 12. Check headlights.
- [ ] Job 13. Check front sidelights and direction indicators.
- [ ] Job 14. Side marker indicators.
- [ ] Job 15. Check rear sidelights, indicators and reverse light.
- [ ] Job 16. Check rear fog lights.
- [ ] Job 17. Check rear number plate light.
- [ ] Job 18. Check luggage compartment light. (WHERE FITTED)
- [ ] Job 19. Check interior light.
- [ ] Job 20. Valet bodywork.
- [ ] Job 21. Vacuum interior.
- [ ] Job 22. Check tyre treads.
- [ ] Job 23. Touch-up paintwork.
- [ ] Job 60. Wiper blades and arms.
- [ ] Job 61. Check windscreen.
- [ ] Job 62. Check floors.
- [ ] Job 78. Adjust headlights.
- [ ] Job 79. Front wheel alignment (tracking).
- [ ] Job 80. Front and rear ride heights.
- [ ] Job 81. Fuel filler cap.
- [ ] Job 82. Change alarm remote batteries.
- [ ] Job 83. Bonnet release.
- [ ] Job 84. Bonnet stay.
- [ ] Job 85. Lubricate locks and hinges.
- [ ] Job 86. Check aerial.
- [ ] Job 87. Check seat mountings.
- [ ] Job 88. Check seat belts.

Every 30,000 miles - Under the Car

First carry out all Jobs listed under earlier Service Intervals as applicable.

- [ ] Job 24. Clean mud traps.
- [ ] Job 36. Hand brake travel.
- [ ] Job 37. Steering rack gaiters.
- [ ] Job 38. Track rod ends gaiters.
- [ ] Job 39. Drain engine oil.
- [ ] Job 40. Change oil filter.
- [ ] Job 41. Pour in fresh oil.
- [ ] Job 42. Check for oil leaks.
- [ ] Job 43. Check front brake pads.
- [ ] Job 44. Check front discs.
- [ ] Job 46. Lubricate front suspension.
- [ ] Job 47. Check steering swivel boots.
- [ ] Job 48. Examine front shock absorber mountings.
- [ ] Job 49. Check front anti-roll bar mountings.
- [ ] Job 50. Examine front suspension unit lower mounting.
- [ ] Job 51. Examine drive shaft gaiters.
- [ ] Job 52. Check front wheelnuts torque.
- [ ] Job 55. Check rear flexible hoses.
- [ ] Job 56. Check rear suspension.
- [ ] Job 57. Lubricate rear suspension.
- [ ] Job 58. Check rear wheelnuts torque.
- [ ] Job 59. Inspect underside.
- [ ] Job 89. Front fuel and brake pipes.
- [ ] Job 90. Exhaust system and mountings.
- [ ] Job 91. Front dampers.
- [ ] Job 92. Steering rack mountings.
- [ ] Job 93. Front subframe mountings and engine mountings.
- [ ] Job 94. Rear brake pipes, fuel pipes and Hydragas suspension pipes.
- [ ] Job 95. Rear dampers.
- [ ] Job 96. Rustproofing under the body.
- [ ] Job 97. Clear drain holes.

Every 30,000 miles - Road Test

First carry out all Jobs listed under earlier Service Intervals as applicable.

- [ ] Job 63. Clean controls.
- [ ] Job 64. Check instruments and controls.
- [ ] Job 65. Throttle and choke cables.
- [ ] Job 66. Road test of brakes and steering.

Date serviced:..

Carried out by:...
Garage Stamp or signature:

Parts/Accessories purchased (date, parts, source) ....
....
....
....

EVERY 33,000 MILES - OR EVERY THIRTY THREE MONTHS, WHICHEVER COMES FIRST

All the Jobs at this Service Interval have been carried forward from earlier Service Intervals and are to be repeated at this service.

Every 33,000 miles - The Engine Bay

- [ ] Job 1. Engine oil level.
- [ ] Job 2. Clutch fluid level.
- [ ] Job 3. Brake fluid level.
- [ ] Job 4. Battery electrolyte.
- [ ] Job 5. Washer reservoir.
- [ ] Job 6. Cooling system level.
- [ ] Job 7. Heater intake box.
- [ ] Job 8. Horn.
- [ ] Job 26. Check HT circuit.
- [ ] Job 27. Check ignition LT circuit.
- [ ] Job 28. Distributor vacuum advance/retard pipe.
- [ ] Job 32. Alternator/fan belt.
- [ ] Job 33. Check air filter.
- [ ] Job 34. OPTIONAL SU carburettor.
- [ ] Job 35. Pipes and hoses.

Every 33,000 miles - Around The Car

- [ ] Job 9. Windscreen washers.
- [ ] Job 10. Windscreen wipers.
- [ ] Job 11. Tyre pressures.
- [ ] Job 12. Check headlights.
- [ ] Job 13. Check front sidelights and direction indicators.
- [ ] Job 14. Side marker indicators.
- [ ] Job 15. Check rear sidelights, indicators and reverse light.
- [ ] Job 16. Check rear fog lights.
- [ ] Job 17. Check rear number plate light.
- [ ] Job 18. Check luggage compartment light. (WHERE FITTED)
- [ ] Job 19. Check interior light.
- [ ] Job 20. Valet bodywork.
- [ ] Job 21. Vacuum interior.
- [ ] Job 22. Check tyre treads.
- [ ] Job 23. Touch-up paintwork.
- [ ] Job 60. Wiper blades and arms.
- [ ] Job 61. Check windscreen.
- [ ] Job 62. Check floors.

Every 33,000 miles - Under the Car

- [ ] Job 24. Clean mud traps.
- [ ] Job 36. Hand brake travel.
- [ ] Job 37. Steering rack gaiters.
- [ ] Job 38. Track rod ends gaiters.
- [ ] Job 39. Drain engine oil.
- [ ] Job 40. Change oil filter.
- [ ] Job 41. Pour in fresh oil.
- [ ] Job 42. Check for oil leaks.
- [ ] Job 43. Check front brake pads.
- [ ] Job 44. Check front discs.
- [ ] Job 46. Lubricate front suspension.
- [ ] Job 47. Check steering swivel boots.
- [ ] Job 48. Examine front shock absorber mountings.
- [ ] Job 49. Check front anti-roll bar mountings.
- [ ] Job 50. Examine front suspension unit lower mounting.

- [ ] Job 51. Examine drive shaft gaiters.
- [ ] Job 52. Check front wheelnuts torque.
- [ ] Job 53. Adjust rear brakes.
- [ ] Job 55. Check rear flexible hoses.
- [ ] Job 56. Check rear suspension.
- [ ] Job 57. Lubricate rear suspension.
- [ ] Job 58. Check rear wheelnuts torque.
- [ ] Job 59. Inspect underside.

Every 33,000 miles - Road Test

First carry out all Jobs listed under earlier Service Intervals as applicable.

- [ ] Job 63. Clean controls.
- [ ] Job 64. Check instruments and controls.
- [ ] Job 65. Throttle and choke cables.
- [ ] Job 66. Road test of brakes and steering.

Date serviced:..

Carried out by: ....
Garage Stamp or signature:

Parts/Accessories purchased (date, parts, source) ....
....
....
....

EVERY 36,000 MILES - OR EVERY THIRTY-SIX MONTHS, WHICHEVER COMES FIRST

All the Service Jobs in the tinted area have been carried forward from earlier service intervals and are to be repeated at this service.

Every 36,000 miles - The Engine Bay

First carry out all Jobs listed under earlier Service Intervals as applicable.

- Job 2. Clutch fluid level.
- Job 3. Brake fluid level.
- Job 4. Battery electrolyte.
- Job 5. Washer reservoir.
- Job 7. Heater intake box.
- Job 8. Horn.
- Job 27. Check ignition LT circuit.
- Job 28. Distributor vacuum advance/retard pipe.
- Job 32. Alternator/fan belt.
- Job 33. Check air filter.
- Job 35. Pipes and hoses.
- Job 67. Cooling system.
- Job 68. Check coolant.
- Job 69. Check water pump.
- Job 70. Fit new spark plugs.
- Job 71. Renew contact breaker points and capacitor.
- Job 72. Ignition timing.
- Job 73. Fuel connections.
- Job 74. Top up carburettor dashpot.
- Job 75. Overhaul carburettor.
- Job 76. Setting the carburettor.
- Job 77. Exhaust emissions.
- Job 98. Breather hoses.
- Job 99. Oil filler cap.
- Job 100. Oil leaks.
- Job 101. Clean radiator.
- Job 102. Check valve clearances.
- Job 103. Clutch stop clearances and mechanism.
- Job 104. Cylinder compressions.

- Job 128. Renew distributor cap and leads.
- Job 129. Float chambers.

Every 36,000 miles - Around the Car

First carry out all Jobs listed under earlier Service Intervals as applicable.

- Job 9. Windscreen washers.
- Job 10. Windscreen wipers.
- Job 11. Tyre pressures.
- Job 12. Check headlights.
- Job 13. Check front sidelights and direction indicators.
- Job 14. Side marker indicators.
- Job 15. Check rear sidelights, indicators and reverse light.
- Job 16. Check rear fog lights.
- Job 17. Check rear number plate light.
- Job 18. Check luggage compartment light. (WHERE FITTED)
- Job 19. Check interior light.
- Job 20. Valet bodywork.
- Job 21. Vacuum interior.
- Job 22. Check tyre treads.
- Job 23. Touch-up paintwork.
- Job 60. Wiper blades and arms.
- Job 61. Check windscreen.
- Job 62. Check floors.
- Job 78. Adjust headlights.
- Job 79. Front wheel alignment (tracking).
- Job 80. Front and rear ride heights.
- Job 81. Fuel filler cap.
- Job 82. Change alarm remote batteries.
- Job 83. Bonnet release.
- Job 84. Bonnet stay.
- Job 85. Lubricate locks and hinges.
- Job 86. Check aerial.
- Job 87. Check seat mountings.
- Job 88. Check seat belts.
- Job 105. Test shock absorbers.
- Job 106. Toolkit and jack.

- Job 130. Rear hubs.

Every 36,000 miles - Under the Car

First carry out all Jobs listed under earlier Service Intervals as applicable.

- Job 24. Clean mud traps.
- Job 36. Hand brake travel.
- Job 37. Steering rack gaiters.
- Job 38. Track rod ends gaiters.
- Job 39. Drain engine oil.
- Job 40. Change oil filter.
- Job 41. Pour in fresh oil.
- Job 42. Check for oil leaks.
- Job 43. Check front brake pads.
- Job 44. Check front discs.
- Job 46. Lubricate front suspension.
- Job 47. Check steering swivel boots.
- Job 48. Examine front shock absorber mountings.
- Job 49. Check front anti-roll bar mountings.
- Job 50. Examine front suspension unit lower mounting.
- Job 51. Examine drive shaft gaiters.
- Job 52. Check front wheelnuts torque.
- Job 53. Adjust rear brakes.
- Job 55. Check rear flexible hoses.
- Job 56. Check rear suspension.
- Job 57. Lubricate rear suspension.
- Job 58. Check rear wheelnuts torque.
- Job 59. Inspect underside.
- Job 89. Front fuel and brake pipes.
- Job 90. Exhaust system and mountings.
- Job 91. Front dampers.
- Job 92. Steering rack mountings.
- Job 93. Front subframe mountings and engine mountings.
- Job 94. Rear brake pipes, fuel pipes and Hydragas suspension pipes.
- Job 95. Rear dampers.
- Job 96. Rustproofing under the body.
- Job 97. Clear drain holes.
- Job 107. Front suspension bushes.
- Job 108. Check steering swivels.
- Job 109. Check steering ball joints and rack.

☐ Job 110. Check steering wheel free play.

☐ Job 111. Front callipers.

☐ Job 112. Rear brake inspection and overhaul.

☐ Job 113. Renew rear brake shoes.

☐ Job 114. Top-up rustproofing.

Every 36,000 miles - Road Test

First carry out all Jobs listed under earlier Service Intervals as applicable.

☐ Job 63. Clean controls.

☐ Job 64. Check instruments and controls.

☐ Job 65. Throttle and choke cables.

☐ Job 66. Road test of brakes and steering.

Date serviced:..

Carried out by: ....
Garage Stamp or signature:

Parts/Accessories purchased (date, parts,

source) ....

....

....

....

N O T E S